THE HACKATHON SURVIVAL GUIDE

MAKE YOUR HACK STAND OUT FROM THE CROWD!

SAMUEL LARSEN-DISNEY

Illustrated by Irma Van den Poel

ISBN: 978-1-7396278-2-9

This book is an accumulation of knowledge imparted to me by leaders, engineers, product owners, user-experience designers, students and friends:

Jonathon Mounty, Adam Wilkinson, Diego Abizaid, Matthew Lee, Rebecca Bayliss, Ruben Casas, Yannis Panagis, Joshua Gabrel, Mateusz Mółka, Krešimir Pehar, Katie Manescu, Ioana Manescu, Joseph Reeve, Mika Tasich, Andrew Mullett, Paul Kiernan, Çelik Köseoğlu, Stefanie Borden, Mathangi Ganesh, Megan Avery, April Selby, Arthur Ceccotti, Oliver Walters, Gitte Porsgaard, Stephen Cager, Steve Davis, Peter Renwick, Rhiain Jenkins, Emmett Wilson, Răzvan Geangu, Guillaume Danis, Magdalena Smith, Adam Sue, Neil Ross, Benjamin Read, Sarmishta Mahendra and of course, Carlota Veal Baschwitz.

You've all helped me on this journey, and it shouldn't go unrecognized. Without your knowledge, wisdom, patience, and encouragement over my career so far, I would not have been able to educate others in the way that I do.

I would particularly like to thank Ryan Gregory, Tessa Breen, and Maurice Banerjee Palmer, who gave their time and energy to ensure that what you are reading represents my best work.

Table of Contents

Preface

In February of 2018, I achieved my first hackathon win. I remember the moment with such clarity. There was a look of bewilderment on my face as representatives from Microsoft handed me an Xbox. The reaction would have been even bigger had I known that the previous night's events would trigger a colossal tangent in my career path.

The journey leading up to this moment started a year prior. I was at university studying computer science and, in all honesty, I wasn't enjoying it. The course, dominated by mathematics and logic, didn't stretch my creative muscles. My good friend and study buddy, Jonathon Mounty, suggested joining an upcoming hackathon at my university. He was more outgoing than me and was the motivator of our friendship group. I had no idea what a hackathon was or how it worked, but the idea of building something together was enough motivation for me to say "Yes!".

During the hack, we stayed up all night building *"BeatStreet"*. *BeatStreet* took your current location and attempted to play music through Spotify related to where you were. The dream was that if you were walking down Abbey Road, the app would play The Beatles. We emulated being at Astley Avenue and "rick-rolled" the entire auditorium during the demo to the judges. I learnt the most crucial element of hacking at this moment: fun. If you're going to stay up all night building something, I think it's vital you sprinkle it with humor and good vibes.

Then we did something stupid. Staying up all night had worn us out. While the pitch to the judges went well, the app was still only half-finished. Without all its features, we were sure we wouldn't win anything. So, like fools, we decided to leave early—big mistake. Within an hour, our phones were blowing up. Every member of the hackathon organizing committee tried to get hold of us. They wanted us to present in the final.

Fast forward a couple of months, we were still kicking ourselves. Johnny turns to me and says, "I think we should try again". Now it just so happened that the largest student-run hackathon "ICHack" was happening at Imperial College two weeks from this point in time. Johnny and I managed to get tickets and vowed that we would stay until the end, regardless of how our hack turned out.

I don't know if you are familiar, but there is a considerable rivalry between the London universities. This time we wouldn't be competing on home turf. It was immediately noticeable when Johnny and I showed up and tried to find two teammates. It was like the moment when you're the last person to be picked for a sports team. No one wanted us, partially due to our lack of skill and partially because of university choice. We ended up forming a team with the only two who were left. However, this ended up being a great thing as one of the two had front-end experience where Johnny and I did not.

With a fair amount of determination, the team stayed up all night. It turned out that we finished the back-end early, and my newfound teammates asked for help with the front-end. This was my first exposure to the world of front-end development.

I was immediately hooked but incredibly inexperienced. So was asking for help left, right and center. What amazes me is that even at 3 AM, I was getting the help I needed from kind-souled mentors who had volunteered their time to help. Who knows if I would still be in front-end development today if I had not received this help?

The brief for this hack was to use Microsoft APIs in an exciting way. We settled on image recognition as something fun and new to try and built a small project called "*Spidentify*". *Spidentify* is an app that takes a photo of a snake or spider and attempts to classify it. We envisioned people using this in the rainforest after being bitten by something nasty. Once the photo was taken and the species identified, in the case that you were going to die, it would direct you to the nearest hospital. A funny fact is that regardless of what you gave it, it would still identify it as either a snake or a spider. During the shortlist demo, we gave it a picture of Donald Trump, and when he came out identified as a snake, the audience burst into laughter.

We took first place in this hack, and I left with more than just an Xbox. I'd made some new mates, but I'd also found a new passion for front-end development. I immediately contacted my graduate scheme coordinator and said I wanted to do front-end in my role. Fast forward to today, and I am still in front-end development as happy as ever.

I hope to do what Johnny did for me. Without these events and projects, I would not have found my passion. In this book, I want to inspire you to attend hackathons, be as creative as possible, and give you my recipe for winning them.

Thanks, Johnny.

THE HACKATHON SURVIVAL GUIDE

CHAPTER ONE

AN INTRODUCTION TO HACKATHONS

In this chapter, we introduce hackathons. We'll first create a standard definition of a hackathon and discover where they all started. We will then investigate the different types and formats before moving on to the benefits of hackathons both to you and those that run them! Finally, we will look at some hackathon success stories.

If you've been to a few hackathons before, you might be tempted to skip this chapter - **I would strongly advise against it!** By understanding why hackathons are run, how they operate, and who the stakeholders are, we can begin to crack the code of how to win them.

What is a Hackathon?

Hackathon comes from a mixture of "hack" and "marathon". A hackathon is an event where teams work on projects (or hacks) centered around a brief or problem statement. Typically, teams are formed of four or five people, but it can be more or less. They can last anywhere from a few hours to a few months (month-long hacks are the real marathons!). Once complete, a panel judges the projects, and there are often prizes for the winning hacks.

I've specifically avoided words like computer programming and software engineering in this definition. Because to me, hackathons are at their best when open to all people. There are many benefits to having a multidisciplinary team from diverse backgrounds. We will discuss this in more detail in Chapter Three.

The Origin of Hackathons

On June 4th 1999, OpenBSD organized an event at a house in Calgary. It aimed to bring developers from across continents into the same room to avoid legal problems exporting cryptographic software from the United States. The word "hackathon" was coined by Niels Provos, who worked at OpenBSD and helped organize the event. It was what you might refer to as a "pure" hackathon. There were no speakers, extra events or specific schedules. The only objective was to aid communication. To get attendees writing code while having the people they might have questions for in the same room.

OpenBSD found the development process had significantly benefited from holding these events and has continued to hold a couple of them every year for the last twenty years.

Hackathons have a reputation for being night-long events. I think this reputation could result from international participants experiencing different levels of jet lag in the early days. OpenBSD developers have joked that they sometimes left events having not experienced any jet lag at all.

In the mid-00s, organizations began to pick up on this kind of event, especially universities. The trend was further accelerated as personal computers became more portable, as it was easier to bring your device to the event. Facebook and Yahoo adopted the event format in 2006. Technology companies noticed that you could use hackathons to attract new talent by running hackathons externally with prizes. Venture capitalists saw it as a great way to spark new products.

As more sponsors got involved, hackathons had more significant funds and supplemented the "pure" hackathon experience with other activities such as workshops, sponsor talks, games tournaments, food, and even karaoke. These extra activities have become staples in the modern hackathon format.

Hackathon Types

Like a "Boggart" from the world of Harry Potter, Hackathons can take on many different forms. They can, however, be grouped into two main types - Internal and External.

Internal

An internal hackathon is one organized by a company for its employers. They focus on creating MVPs for new products, adding experimental new features to existing products or improving internal processes. They usually take place during work hours, and, as the company is paying for employee time, briefs typically include business value as a necessity. Internal hackathons also do wonders for company culture as they offer an excellent opportunity for colleagues to meet people from other parts of the business.

Example Briefs for Internal Hacks:

- Build an app that uses our new transaction API.
- Create a product that helps colleagues meet while working remotely.

Example Judging Criteria:

- **Business Value:** How well does this solve the problem or adhere to the brief?
- **Monetization Strategy:** How will the product make money?
- **Implementation:** How skillfully was the project created? How appropriate is the project's technology stack?
- **Realistic Capability:** How user-friendly (or accessible) is the end product?
- **Presentation:** How engaging was the presentation? How well was the idea was conveyed? How informative was the product demo?

One important rule to clarify with your company is the intellectual property around a hackathon idea. If the hackathon occurs during work hours and your employer is paying you, they will most likely own the intellectual property surrounding anything you build on the day.

External

External hackathons are those where the organizers invite members outside of their institution to participate. These could be organized by university students, charities, large or small companies. The reasons why external hackathons are run varies far more than internal. While business value can sometimes still be applicable, external hack briefs can focus on non-monetary goals such as improving education, sustainability, or making the internet more accessible.

Example Briefs for External Hacks:

- Build an app that helps educate people on online safety with gamification.
- Use our datasets to raise awareness of rising sea levels.
- Use Microsoft APIs to create tools that help local communities affect by earthquakes.

Example Judging Criteria:

- **Uniqueness:** Is the solution the first of its kind? How innovative is the solution?
- **Viability:** Is the idea realistic? Does it adequately solve the problem?
- **Implementation:** How much skill was needed to create the project? How appropriate is the project's technology stack?
- **Presentation:** How engaging was the presentation? How well was the idea was conveyed? How informative was the product demo?

At the back of this book, you'll find example hackathon challenges complete with judging criteria so you can practice!

Hackathon Formats

Hackathons can be onsite, online or hybrid. Let's explore these types in a little bit more details and identify the differences:

Onsite

An onsite hackathon is the classic hackathon experience. In this format, everyone participating attends in person. They are usually the shortest format as organizers also have to deal with the cost of venue hire. Most last less than three days.

An onsite hackathon kicks off with an opening ceremony. Here you will be introduced to the challenges and hear words from any sponsors. Upon the ceremony's conclusion, the hack officially begins. This is where it starts to get intense! Due to the shorter time limit, attendees will generally work on their idea through the night.

As you might imagine, working on a project solidly for two or three days isn't very healthy, so events are usually scattered throughout the duration. These might include technical talks from mentors or sponsors on particular technologies or frameworks, meditation classes, or late-night karaoke. Mealtimes are a great opportunity to step back from your idea and socialize. Sponsors often cover the cost of food and, as it's free for participants, you'll normally see a stampede of people heading in the direction of food when it's time.

YOU FRONT-END OR BACK-END?
I WILL UPEND THIS DRINK IN YOUR FACE UNLESS YOU MOVE

Mentors are normally on hand if you require technical help throughout the night. If you require clarification around the challenge, it's as easy as asking the sponsor who set it up—co-locating means that you can get the answers you need faster. It also means that you can pitch to the judges live. This can be really helpful as you can see how judges are reacting to your presentation and pivot if you need to on the fly (more on this in Chapter 10).

The time between judging and winner announcement is normally small - winners are announced in the closing ceremony a couple of hours after judging. If you win, more often than not, you can leave with your prize that very same day!

In my professional opinion, Onsite hackathons are the best place to begin your hackathon journey. They are typically more structured than other formats, which can be beneficial if you are participating for the first time.

Online

Online hackathons have the lowest barrier to entry. You can roll straight out of bed, open up your laptop and participate! Online hackathons are often international, allowing you to meet people from all over the world. Due to their openness and ease of access, this format attracts the most competitors.

Online hacks are typically longer in duration than onsite and can last anywhere from a day to a few months. This extra time is convenient as communication can be slower. Your team might be distributed across time zones. It can also help you feel a little less time-pressured and more relaxed.

Due to the typically increased number of participants, online hacks have more submissions than other formats. And a more extended judging period must ensue. As you can imagine, it would be challenging for the judges to hear each pitch in person, so instead, online hackathons typically focus on more extensive submissions (Submissions are explored in detail in Chapter 9!). Submissions are shared publicly for other attendees and the judges to review when the deadline passes.

Just because the hack is online doesn't mean that there aren't any events you can attend! Game servers are set up, talks and workshops are presented via Zoom, and help is given via Slack or Discord. However, there is one serious downside - **you have to supply your own pizza!**

Hybrid

Hybrid hackathons attempt to combine the best of both worlds with an in-person event space for those who want it and the ability to participate entirely remotely. How these operate is a little less formalized, and you will see organizers pick and mix parts of the onsite and online events to create something that works for participants.

You might be wondering where you find the right hackathon for you. **Don't worry!** We will cover this in Chapter 2.

Benefits of Hackathons

Hackathons provide some great benefits to attendees and companies alike. Let's take a look at these in detail.

Attendees

Whether you win the hack or not, there are plenty of benefits to being involved in a hackathon.

- **Learn Something New:** Hackathons are a great way to "learn by doing". Most events have mentors on-hand to help you learn the skills you need to finish your project. If you already know what you're doing, hackathons can provide you with the space to try that new tool you haven't had the time to use yet.

- **Escape:** In our day jobs, it's impossible to reach our full creative potential all of the time. We might be slowed down by politics, design constraints, legal requirements, test code coverage, logic that just won't work, technology set-up issues, other teams, the list goes on. Hackathons provide a way to get out of those situations and flex those creative muscles. Remind yourself that you can be an innovative machine when there's nothing in the way.
- **Expand Your Network:** How often do you have hundreds of people from your field in the same room? Hackathons provide a rare opportunity to meet people like you. Speak to people doing the job you want to pursue, or investigate that company that interests you. You'll know you're doing it right if you leave the event with a handful of LinkedIn connections. These could be future employers or people you might look to work with in the future!
- **Make Friends:** Nothing brings people together like building something together!
- **Win a prize:** Though not guaranteed, you might come away with a prize as well as your cool project! This could be money, vouchers, or something physical like a piece of technology.

It's important to remember that all the above happen at every hackathon, but you can miss these opportunities if you don't take them. **Challenge yourself** to learn that new technology, meet people in the industry or talk to that stranger hacking next to you!

As a student, there are some additional benefits:

- **Reinforce Your Learnings:** Depending on your course, you might find your curriculum dominated by theory. Hackathons allow you to put your learnings into practice, which could help your understanding of a subject.
- **Fill your CV/Personal Site:** Finishing your education and immediately starting your job hunt can be difficult if you don't have work experience demonstrating your technical ability. Hackathons provide a way to add a relevant project to your CV or website with minimal time investment. Hack projects can also demonstrate team-working, leadership and even presentation skills!
- **Job Offer or Fast-Track Interview:** Often, event sponsors are tech companies actively recruiting. Most, if not all, of these companies, will have graduate schemes or internships. In some hacks, the reward is tied to recruitment. They might offer the winner a fast-track to interview or even a job offer!

Companies

Over 80% of the Fortune 100 run hackathons, with over 50% of those companies making them regular occurrences. It is clear by their frequency that these companies recognize that hackathons are powerful tools for innovation. Let's look at what companies have to gain.

- **Test New Software Products:** Hackathons can be a forum for testing new products. User testing can be an expensive endeavor. If you are trying to keep costs down, you can create a challenge that requires participants to use the product you want to test. You can find bugs and receive feedback on the tool, with the only cost being a prize for the winner - it's a no-brainer!
- **Product Development (Internal Only):** Much like OpenBSD's first hack, hackathons can see an existing product's growth

accelerate if it is made to be the focus. It also might be an opportunity to explore alternative avenues or experimental products. Hackathons present an opportunity to create a proof of concept to prove an idea in minimal time.

- **Improve Company Culture (Internal Only):** Hackathons provide an opportunity for colleagues to meet, learn from each other, and explore ideas that they usually wouldn't. All of these contribute to excellent company culture.
- **Recruitment (External Only):** For tech companies, it's essential to have a steady talent pipeline as average tenure within the tech industry is less than two years. External hackathons provide a great way to advertise your company to potential employees.

Hackathon Success Stories

For most, a hack project's development ends with the event. However, some take hackathon projects and turn them into profitable futures. Let's take a look at Appetas, Carousell and GroupMe, all of which have earned teams millions of dollars.

Appetas

The pair behind Appetas created their project from a shared hatred of restaurant websites. They built a simple website creation engine that pulls data from public APIs to create stunning, user-friendly, functional restaurant websites that look good on any device. The idea took first place at the 2012 AngelHack competition, and the team earned a $25,000 prize. After the hack, Keller Smith and Curtis Fonger raised a further investment of $120,000 to pursue the project and build out the platform. In May 2014, Google approached the company and bought Appetas for an undisclosed amount. Data on Google's acquisitions suggests that this amount is likely to be higher than $10,000,000.

Carousell

Lucas Ngoo and Quek Siu Rui created Carousell at their very first hackathon! Carousell is a community marketplace that facilitates buying and selling anything you own, whether that's clothes, books, even cars and houses! The idea took first place at the Startup Weekend 2012 Hackathon in Singapore. Over the years that followed, they have successfully turned their project into a business with $287,000,000 in funding to date and have offices across the globe.

GroupMe

Thanks to Facebook and WhatsApp, group chats are a normality today. But back in 2011, if you wanted to send multiple people the same message, you would have to copy and paste! Jared Hecht and Steve Martocci were attending Tech Crunch Disrupt at the time and wanted to change this nightmare. They built GroupMe, which creates private SMS groups between multiple people, friends, colleagues or family. The team themselves started using it as soon as they built it. This team didn't win the hackathon (they left with an honorable mention), but they believed in their idea so much that they left their employment to pursue it. They raised $850,000 in funding and, in less than a year, were acquired by Skype for $80,000,000.

It's worth noticing that these success stories have really small teams. This is a great thing to keep in mind if you are below the maximum team size and worried that this means you're less likely to win - **success at hackathons does not correlate to team size**.

Mission Accomplished!

You got through chapter one. Nice job! If there is anything I want you to take away from this chapter, it's excitement. A hackathon could be the way you meet your best friend, find a job you love, or perhaps spark the idea behind the start-up that makes you millions.

In the next chapter, we will help you find a hackathon where you will excel. So what are you waiting for? Turn the page!

CHAPTER TWO

So, after Chapter 1, you're hyped to attend a hackathon, but you don't know where to look? This chapter has you covered! We will identify the best ways to find different types of hackathons. We'll also talk about what to look out for before applying. Finally, if you can't find a hack that suits you, we will briefly discuss the first steps to creating your own.

In the last chapter, we identified a trifecta of different hackathon types. One of those types likely appealed to you more than the rest based on your personality. Keep that type in mind, and feel free to jump to the relevant section. But before you do, probably best to read the following section on hackathon considerations!

Hackathon Considerations

When browsing for hackathons, consider the following:

- **Your Interests:** Does the problem statement excite you? If you're going to spend a chunk of time intensely ideating to come up with imaginative and creative solutions, you want to be enthusiastic.
- **The Rules:** Most hackathons have a set of criteria your project entry needs to meet to qualify. Check that your age, student status (or lack thereof) and technical experience doesn't disqualify you. Even if you do qualify, ask yourself if you are the target demographic that this hackathon is targeting. You don't want to feel out of place!
- **The Number of Participants:** If the participant count is low, you might find it harder to find teammates. However, it also makes it easier to get help from mentors when you need it as they are less stretched.

  I find 100 to 300 people to be a good size!

- **The Length:** Long and short hacks both provide different experiences. Quick hacks can be pretty intense as you are really up against the clock. Longer hacks will usually be completed alongside work or study and can be quite draining as a result, so consider this before embarking on the adventure!
- **The Prizes:** This shouldn't matter if you are here to learn. Knowledge is worth infinite money. If, however, you are "in it to win it", then check the prizes. The more prizes on offer, the more chances you will win one.

Some of the best prizes are not money at all! One of the best prizes I have ever received was the opportunity to present at a developer conference in California! Networking, coding and sun! What more could you want?

Now that we know what to look out for let's find that hack!

Online & Hybrid

Since the COVID pandemic began, the number of hackathons being hosted online or as a hybrid has gone up like crazy! You now have plenty of choices when deciding which kind of hack you want to participate in. There are hacks on web design, cryptocurrencies, augmented reality, game development - the list goes on! Take your time to find the one that suits you. Don't compromise. You will find what you're looking for if you're patient.

There are many different websites where you can find an online hackathon to participate in. Two of the most popular are Devpost and Major League Hacking. Let's explore these in detail.

Devpost

Website: devpost.com

The number one online source for finding remote hackathons is Devpost.com. Companies like Amazon, Facebook, Microsoft, IBM, Intel, Cisco, Atlassian, and Twitter use Devpost to host their hackathons.

One of the great things about Devpost is that it can double as a project portfolio. Projects you complete on the platform all appear on your Devpost portfolio. If you're short on time and need to demonstrate some of your work, sharing your Devpost portfolio can can be a quick way to demonstrate your skills.

Devpost shows you ongoing hacks and upcoming ones. I find it's always best to lean towards the upcoming ones; otherwise, you are starting at a disadvantage as other teams will have had more time to produce a project. Joining even just a few days in advance of a hack starting is more than enough time to prepare so don't let that put you off.

Once you've chosen a hack on the platform that piques your interest, join it by hitting the big "register" button! As the event approaches, you should receive an email with a link to the hackathon Slack or Discord. Most hackathon communication platforms open "teammate and networking" social channels early so you can start finding a team. Be sure to enter these ahead of the hack, so you don't have any technical difficulties on the start day. There are more Devpost related tips in *Chapter 10: The submission*.

It should be noted that Devpost is not exclusively for remote events, and you may be able to find in-person hackathons through the platform. Most in-person hacks require an additional signup on another platform, so be sure to read all the information on the hackathon's page.

Major League Hacking

Website: mlh.io

If you're already in full-time employment, this isn't for you as Major League Hacking (or MLH for short) organizes hackathon leagues specifically for students or those that have just graduated.

MLH operates hackathons in yearly seasons. Attendees can participate in any of the two-hundred weekend-long events they host during the year, most of which are digital. MLH has distilled hackathons into a great formula - they are some of the most organized hackathons you can attend with dedicated mentors and on-hand friendly staff who organize the events.

When browsing for hackathons on MLH's site, you can see up to two month's worth of upcoming events, so you have plenty of time to decide which events you want to attend.

A final thought on remote hacks....

Just because a hackathon is remote doesn't mean your team has to be! If you are hacking with friends, why not invite them over and work at the dinner table together? Pizza party? Donuts?

Onsite

Now that we have investigated online hackathons, let's turn our attention to the other type - onsite.

University Students

Most universities have tech societies that run hackathons. These can be a great way to enter the hackathon scene. You can meet fellow students with shared interests and perhaps even make a whole new group of friends – a "whirlwind" of shared experiences like hackathons tend to bring people closer together.

Don't restrict yourself to your own university - nothing is stopping you from applying to a hackathon at another university that you can visit. Oh! Also, it's good to note that you can normally still attend university hacks up to 12 months after you graduate!

Looking Internally

Most large tech corporations host hackathons. Usually, the brief or problem statement is restricted to ensure that the projects serve a business purpose. This might enforce the tech you can use or limit the ideas you can explore. But this doesn't mean they aren't fun experiences!

Keep an ear open in company meetings and an eye on internal communications such as email or Slack, as this is where they most likely will be announced.

If you're looking to be a little more creative (or escape your colleagues!), then you may need to look outside of work.

Looking Externally

Outside of work, you may be able to find a hackathon by looking for local events. Two great places to look are Eventbrite and Meetup:

Eventbrite

Website: eventbrite.com

Eventbrite is a website that allows users to browse, create and promote local events. A quick search for "hack" or "hackathon" often yields a few results. If you're open to remote hackathons, you can also increase the distance you are searching in and see if any remote hackathons from further afield show up.

Fun fact! Eventbrite has a free API. Why not create a project that finds hackathons for you automagically? Yes, automagically is a word.

Meetup

Website: meetup.com

Meetup is a service used to organize online groups that host in-person and virtual events for people with similar interests. Here you can join a group related to a technology you are interested in and receive multiple invites to related hackathons throughout the year as a result!

If your company doesn't run hackathons and you can't find one externally that suits you, maybe you should start one instead? Let's take a look at how!

Starting a Hack

When you are unable to find a hackathon that piques your interest then you wouldn't be the first to start your own! A whole separate book could be written on organizing and running hackathons, so instead, we will focus on some of the key considerations:

- **Present an actionable plan, not an idea:** Whether you are holding the hackathon internally or externally, you'll need help! When getting others involved, you'll find it easier if you have a plan of action rather than just an idea.
- **Keep the theme(s) accessible:** Consider your attendees when coming up with hackathon themes and problem statements. Will they have the required technical skills to build a relevant project in the timeframe? Also, make sure your themes are broad enough that attendees can take it in multiple different directions. There's nothing worse than numerous teams pitching the same idea at the end of the hack!
- **Have a jam-packed schedule:** Ensure your agenda includes workshops, ice-breakers and (of course) food! This helps break up the hacking and stops attendees from burning out. It also helps keep them motivated and happy!
- **Find sponsorship:** If you are not running the hackathon as part of a company, you might need some funding if you don't want to break the bank! A great place to start would be to contact local tech companies actively recruiting. They might exchange financing for a spotlight on their company.
- **Ensure your attendees are supported:** Hackathons work best when attendees can get help when they need it. Help them overcome difficulties with subject matter experts on hand as mentors. This could be technical issues or simply sound boarding to help carve out an idea.
- **Think about prize distribution:** If your attendees will be of mixed ability, it can sometimes be better not to have an overall winner but instead have multiple categories within which to compete.

Hackathons and Monetary Value

If your reason for competing in a hackathon is motivated by prizes, you might want to calculate whether it is worth your time and, if so, how much time? How you determine what is worth your time is, of course, personal to you but comparing the prize value to your annual salary can help you.:

$$\frac{annual\ salary}{hours\ you\ work\ a\ year} = hourly\ rate$$

$$\frac{prize\ money}{hourly\ rate} = hours\ you'd\ work\ for\ the\ same\ amount$$

Here we first calculate your hourly rate. We then divide the prize amount by your hourly rate to get an estimation on the number of hours you would work for the same amount. If the number of hours is greater than the amount of time you can commit at the hack, this means it's worth your time. If the number is drastically smaller, you might be less likely to invest your time as you could make more in your day job. A small number might also be an indication that you're overqualified.

This calculation does not take tax into account. It also does not exclude the possibility of you losing. As such, use it only as a guesstimate.

Let's take a salary of $50,000 USD and hackathon with a prize amount of $1000 and run through the calculation:

$$\frac{\$50,000}{2048\ hours} = \$24.4/hr$$

$$\frac{\$1000}{\$24.4/hr} = 40\ hours$$

I don't endorse hacking exclusively for monetary gain. As we investigated in Chapter One, there are many reasons to participate. Money and prizes are a tiny part of that and are the only benefit not guaranteed!

Time for a Pit Stop!

Enthusiasm? **Check!** Hackathon Identified? **Check!** Registered? **Check!**

You've now completed all the pre-planning required before attending a hackathon - great job! We still have a long way to go on this journey, starting with your team. A hackathon project won't come alive without a team around it and, in the next chapter, we will discuss what you should look for in your teammates and where to find them!

CHAPTER THREE

YOUR TEAM

A hackathon team is made up of individuals with different strengths experiences, backgrounds, and ways of thinking. Your team's composition can drastically change your team's ability and the kinds of projects you can tackle.

People often forget this when thrown into a room with strangers. They huddle with their folks, who all have the same skillset because meeting new people can be intimidating.

As we discussed in Chapter One, working on a hack with someone is a great way to meet new people in the industry. If you stick with the people you know, you may miss this opportunity, so I implore you to branch out.

Useful Technical Skills

Most projects will, at a *minimum*, need two people, one with Front-end experience and one with Back-end experience:

Front-End Experience

Front-End refers to the building of user interfaces. Experience in Front-End means you are comfortable bringing the visual elements of a hack to life. The Front-End of a project can take many forms, including websites, mobile apps and native applications.

Examples of front-end experience may include knowledge of web frameworks like NextJS or Gatsby, UI libraries like ReactJS, mobile app development frameworks like Flutter, React Native, or animation libraries like Framer Motion. Common languages include HTML, JavaScript and CSS.

Back-End Experience

Back-End refers to the parts of a website or app that you can't see. Experience in the Back-End means you are comfortable handling requests from the front-end and organizing and storing data required by your project.

Examples of Back-End experience may include HTTP servers, sockets, databases or authentication. Common languages include Python, Java and JavaScript.

Don't have either of these skills? Or, want to try something different? **Don't worry.** Hackathons are a great place to learn new skills! Take something that interests you from the list above and express your enthusiasm for it. In these scenarios, it's best to team up with someone else. Doing so makes you less likely to make silly mistakes and helps you learn faster. We'll talk more about this later.

If your team possesses both front-end and back-end experience, you will have everything you need to build a functional app or website. But, some additional roles can elevate the project - User Experience Designers and Graphic Designers can take your hack from good to great.

User Experience Design

A UX designer will investigate the behavior and habits of users to identify ways to improve the experience of using the project. This role shines in longer hacks with time to iterate based on user feedback.

While the role of a UX designer can be incredibly varied, their primary objective is to help products provide meaningful and relevant experiences. A UX designer might identify essential user flows, create a design language system and wireframes, perform user testing, highlight accessibility issues, and mock-up any parts of your application you don't have time to build.

In some instances, UX designers can also submit a hackathon project all by themselves without Front-End and Back-End engineers. Using tools like Figma or Sketch, they can create high-fidelity prototypes that perfectly convey an idea. This, combined with a presentation, can be a powerful way to pitch a project to the judges.

If you are a UX designer and at a hackathon with engineers, I would advise against storming ahead without them. By teaming up with engineers, you have the chance of getting to a deployed application in the hack. Something you are unlikely to achieve on your own.

Graphic Design

Nothing elevates a hack project like a brand. A visual identity consistent throughout the product, presentation, and submission, can help tie everything together. Someone with graphic design know-how can help define that visual identity by creating a logo, product messaging, color and typography combinations.

I'm going to stereotype here, but graphic and UX designers can also make **kick-ass** and **visually-striking** presentations! Having one of these to look over your slide deck can help you communicate your project better to the judges.

Useful Soft Skills

Aside from technical skills, soft skills can be beneficial too:

- **Presentational skills:** At the end of the hackathon, you will need to articulate what you have built to the judges—having someone in your team who is a confident public speaker can make your project stand out.
- **Professional communication skills:** Most hackathons include a written submission. Hack projects such as websites and apps will also require text to help communicate ideas to users. Someone who possesses communication skills will help your project come across better on paper and a screen.

- **Problem-solving skills:** At its core, a hackathon is a process of finding an innovative solution to a problem statement. Someone with an "out-of-the-box" thinking attitude might help you find the perfect hackathon idea quicker.
- **Teamwork skills:** Teamwork makes the dream work! Being a clear communicator and taking the time to listen to your teammates will help avoid confusion and keep everyone on the same page.

Now that we understand what types of skills we might want in our team, let's look at where we might find them.

Finding a Team

The first step to finding a team is identifying the roles you resonate with from the section above. Advertise which bases you can cover and what functions you are looking for in your teammates. It would help if you didn't oversell yourself. Make sure you feel confident that you can handle the skills you commit to, as your team may be relying on you to lead that domain.

What if I don't have any experience?

If you're planning on tackling a new skill, be sure to buddy up with someone with a little more experience! Be clear about what you want to learn, so you have a better chance of achieving it.

What if I am a "Jack of all trades"?

If you are lucky enough to be skilled in more than one area of software development, you can be a tremendous asset to the team! The trick in this position is not to over-commit. Choose the role you want to work in and offer yourself as support in any others.

YOUR FIRE-BREATHING EXPERIENCE WILL REALLY COME IN HANDY FOR OUR PRESENTATION!
UH, YEAH ABOUT THAT...

The Intro Message

Most hackathons have a forum for meeting and creating teams. Be sure to send a message there as early as you can. Here's a template for your first message:

That last line might sound a little cheesy but showing enthusiasm is essential. People should be looking for individuals who are invested in the hackathon.

You might be in the fortunate position of having an idea you want to work on already prepared. This is a great thing to voice in your opening message, but keep it short and sweet. An elevator pitch will work far better at enticing other teammates than an essay!

If you still don't find what you're looking for after firing off a message in the available social channels, you can always fall back on friends or colleagues. Working with people you know means you have more of a guarantee of ability, but you also lose some networking opportunities and chances to make friends.

Upskill Like a Pro

Hackathons provide the perfect opportunity to learn a new skill! In this section, we will take a look at some tips on how to learn fast and teach well.

Tips for Learning Fast:

Some common methods for learning fast and smart at hackathons include:

- **Pair Programming:** When working on the same part of the project in a group, you can "learn by doing" with pair programming. Pair programming is a tremendous *agile* process often used when two software engineers work on the same feature. Have the experienced individual walk through building a feature while the newbie implements the changes. Pairing opens up a forum where you can discuss how the feature technically works whilst feeling like everyone is actively contributing.
- **Shadow:** If pair programming doesn't work for you, you could instead shadow an individual as they implement a feature. Ask them to describe what they are doing as they do it and ask as many questions as you can to increase your learning.
- **Know When to Ask for Help:** You might feel like you are being a burden by asking for help again and again. While you should definitely try and solve things on your own before asking, sometimes a five-minute conversation can save you 3 hours of head-scratching. Any good mentor will know this. Timebox your problem-solving. If time runs out and you haven't made any progress - find a mentor and get a hint!
- **Be a Smart Googler:** When googling for resources to aid your learning, use quotes. Quotes make Google search for an exact

match which means that only websites containing the phrase or word will appear. This can slim down the search results you have to sift through to help you find what you're looking for quicker.

- **Don't Skim-Read Documentation:** When you feel like you're up against the clock, it is almost natural to speed through software documentation without really absorbing it. If you're learning how to use new technology and it's not working, returning to the documentation and giving it a good read should be your first port of call.
- **Explore GitHub:** If you're working with new technology, you might be struggling to get the code implementation right. However, you're unlikely to be the first one to have experienced this issue. You can search open-source code on GitHub to find the usage of packages or languages. If you're looking for the use of an NPM package for example, you can search for the package name and limit your search to JavaScript files. This should net you some useful results!

Everyone has their way of learning. We can use some common approaches within technology, but it's always best to experiment and work out what is best for you.

Say Thank You!

Always be grateful and patient with anyone that takes the time to teach you. They've invested time in you! The skills you learn here might be the ones that help you land your next job. It also can make someone's day so what's stopping you?!

I was first introduced to ReactJS at a hackathon. It sparked a passion that continues to shape my career. Imagine if that person hadn't taken the time to teach me?

Tips for Teaching Effectively

If you're planning on taking someone under your wing, consider these tips:

- **Keep it casual and fun:** This is not school. This is not an exam. Treat the individual with patience and understanding. Make it fun! Show your passion and ooze enthusiasm.
- **Check-in often:** If you're more experienced than your team members, you might be doing most of the talking. Please don't assume that silence means they are absorbing everything. Check-in as you go; it's as easy as asking "do you understand it all so far?". You wouldn't build a house with flawed foundations; make sure the baseline knowledge is solid.
- **Let them get hands-on:** Some people learn better by applying their learning. Show the individual how to do something once and ask them to repeat it.
- **Don't forget best practices entirely:** Remember that building something in a hack can be rushed or "hacky" and may not be the best way to do something in the real world. When you add something that you wouldn't usually, point this out to the newbie and explain why to aid their understanding of the tools you are using.
- **Go slow to go fast:** If you are experienced, you might find that by taking a little time early on to help teach, you can empower the rest of the team to do some of the work you might find a little mundane. Teaching and subsequently delegating will allow you to focus on the more challenging parts of the project that require a more skilled individual.

If you are volunteering your time to teach someone - Thank you! Hopefully, you will find what I have; teaching is gratifying! Teaching is also a great way to reinforce your own learning.

FELLOWSHIP ASSEMBLED!
And just like that, we've transformed from a lone wolf into a band of confident adventurers.
Armed with technical, design and collaboration skills, your team is about to become a creative machine.
We just need something to focus on...

In this chapter, we're going to explore idea generation and validation. Before we do that, though, let's talk about one crucial trait you require - *patience*.

You might turn up to hack with an app idea. If the challenges are released ahead of time, it can be too tempting to start getting creative before you arrive! Try and resist the urge as additional criteria are often announced during the opening ceremony, or you might find that the challenge wasn't what you thought. If you already have your heart set on an idea, but it doesn't quite match the brief, you might try and bend it to fit. This can put you at a disadvantage as the judges might notice it's preconceived. If you're "in it to win it", be patient and wait until you have the brief in your hands and a team around you to generate ideas.

In the past, I have attended hackathons where the challenges were released two weeks ahead of the event, but they then changed them on the starting day. Please don't assume they are set in stone the first time you see them.

The Making of a Good Idea

A good idea boils down to three core concepts: an idea's simplicity, its relation to you, and its potential. Let's look at each of these.

The Simplicity Rule

You know you have a good idea when you can explain it in simple terms. If the concept takes half an hour to explain, you will struggle to convince your team to participate, and when you come to present it to the judges, you may lose their attention before you get to demo the project!

Be sure you can distil it into an elevator pitch. An elevator pitch is a short description of your project that can be used to explain the concept to anyone in a short amount of time. Having an elevator pitch is something you will need to validate your product in the last section of this chapter. If you struggle to do this, this suggests the idea might be too complex.

The Relational Rule

Keep the problem statement and idea related to you. Firstly, it helps your motivation throughout the event; you will be more invested if you solve a problem you experience. Secondly, a personal connection makes conveying a story about the idea's origin to the judges easier.

The power of this is best shown with an example; the following snippet is from Yannis Panagis' and my hackathon presentation for "Esri's Hack for a Sustainable Future":

"While playing around with Chrome's lighthouse accessibility tool to improve our personal websites, we realized far more data was transferred when the page loaded than we thought. Each visit sent about 4MB of data. This might not sound like a lot, but megabytes can quickly turn into gigabytes if you have a large quantity of site traffic. Every byte sent requires energy, which in turn produces carbon dioxide and other greenhouse gases. But it isn't just us building and visiting sites - there are billions of people and pages on the web. It was then that we realized that, somehow, the tool that we love most ~the internet~ was doing a lot of damage to our planet. This led us to ask the question - how can we fix this?!"

Hopefully, you can see how quickly you can amplify something related to you into a real-world problem statement and give off the feeling of more investment in the issue.

The Potential Rule

Make sure you choose an idea that has the possibility of being something grander outside of the hackathon. As we saw in Chapter One, ideas found at hacks can go on to be worth millions of dollars. But potential can be about more than just money. Perhaps your idea has the chance to help people or communities?

At the start of a hack, people tend to be a little secretive around their idea for fear that someone might steal it. I'd encourage you not to be like this but instead, be open to people asking about your idea. You will gain a wealth of feedback from individuals that might go on to shape your product! I would also like to note that in the 50+ hackathons I have attended, I have never seen a hackathon project stolen, and if a hack idea was taken, it would be immediately evident to the judges.

Idea Generation

Two of the best idea generation methods I've come across can be borrowed directly from the design sprint format.

A design sprint is a week-long workshop for answering business questions through design and prototyping. Due to the short timeframe of these events, you usually have less than a day to come up with an idea - comparable to hackathons. Let's look at two of their idea generation sessions that are normally run as part of a design sprint - Lightning Demos and Crazy Eights.

Lightning Demos

Lightning demos are all about finding comparable problems and their solutions. The perfect hackathon solution may already be out there, just waiting to be re-contextualized or repurposed. You can find these in two easy steps:

1. Gather your team together and ask the following questions - are there other industries with similar problems? If so, which ones and what was the problem?
2. Pull out your laptops and have your team research how industries solved these problems. Can the same method be applied to the problem statement at the hackathon? If yes, then congratulations! You've just discovered a hack idea!

Now for the "lightning". Have each team member give thirty-second pitches on their discoveries.

Crazy Eights

Crazy Eights is an idea generation method we can take directly from design sprints. It is a quick sketching process that challenges you to create eight distinct ideas in eight minutes. The idea is to generate a wide variety of solutions instead of focusing on any single idea.

This process might feel like a foreign concept to those who haven't tried it before, particularly those that don't like drawing. Remind those participating that the drawings are intended to be "rough" and do not by any means need to be perfect or beautiful. The only thing they have to do is communicate an idea.

The ideas don't need to be excellent. The more "out there" and impractical, the better! The weird and wacky ideas are usually the ones that lead to the most creative solutions. Hence the "Crazy" in "Crazy Eights".

Ready to get started? Perform the following steps:

In a group of four, this process will generate thirty-two ideas! Go around your group and give every team member a chance to talk through their sketches.

Once you start generating ideas, you might have a good idea early on. Again, be patient. Don't jump on the first good idea; there might be another one right around the corner that you would miss if you stopped. Instead, timebox idea generation and work up until the last minute.

Validating Ideas

You should now have plenty of ideas swimming around the group. Let's turn our attention to how we can validate them to find those that will take you on to win.

While whittling down ideas, I encourage using "Yes and..." thinking. The "Yes, and..." thinking is a method stolen from improvisational comedy that fosters a performer to listen to what another participant has said and then expand upon it. Saying "Yes" encourages people to internalize ideas and be more receptive to those proposed by others. Rather than quickly shutting an idea down, it would be best to initially accept it, enabling the discussion to expand on the idea without hindrance. Saying "and" helps people steer clear from directly changing the suggested idea and instead build on what has already been proposed.

Ask the Big Questions

When you think you've stumbled on a great idea, make sure that it answers "yes" to the following questions:

- **Does it fit the challenge brief?** You're about to spend a chunk of time turning your idea into a reality. Be sure that your product applies to the problem statement or challenge and hits any relevant judging criteria.
- **Is it technically feasible?** With the time you have available and the skills within your team, is it possible to turn the idea into a

product? If the answer is "no", can you fake parts of the application to help demonstrate the idea?

- **Is the idea an MVP?** There's nothing wrong with having an idea with lots of features, but do you need all of those features to demonstrate it? If the answer is "no", try to scale back any additional features to leave you with a Minimal Viable Product. It doesn't mean you won't implement the extras if you have time; it just means that you will prioritize the most critical features first.
- **Who are your competitors?** Search for any similar products on the market and identify competitors. If you find any, be sure you understand how your idea is different, and make sure it is not a direct copy.

Pitch the Idea to Peers

You have to present your idea at the end of the hackathon, but it can also be beneficial to pitch it right at the beginning too. Gather some friends, explain the challenge and give them your idea's elevator pitch. See how they react to the idea, and listen to any feedback. You don't have to agree with any of it if you don't want to, but you might find some valid questions or concerns that you'll need to address to make the idea work.

Not everyone you talk to will be right. My partner will hate me for using her as an example here, but I like to run all ideas past her when participating in a hackathon. Every hackathon idea I pursue that has gone on to win first place, she has disliked. It now forms part of my idea validation checklist - Does she dislike it? Yes? It must be a good idea then!

SO, MY PITCH. HERE WE GO.
MY IDEA ACTUALLY CAME TO ME AFTER AN INTERACTION WITH MY SISTER-IN-LAW. SHE HAD UNFORTUNATELY BEEN SCAMMED INTO BUYING 40 PACKS OF DIET PILLS.
A SHAM, OF COURSE! I ALWAYS TELL HER: YOU'RE PERFECT THE WAY YOU ARE, AND A NUMBER ON THE SCALE WON'T MAKE YA HAPPY!
ANYWAYS, SHE WAS STUCK WITH ALL PILLS, AND HOO BOY, WAS MY BROTHER NOT HAPPY. THE MONEY WAS GO TO THEIR ONLY CHILD'S

Quick Prototype

When the hack is over a long period (e.g. weeks or months), it can be best to try and build a smaller prototype of the project first. The prototype could be made entirely in design software like Figma without a Back-End or Front-End as that would be all you need to demonstrate a user journey.

You can present the prototype to peers and see how they respond. If possible, let them be hands-on with the prototype rather than guiding them through it. Watching them play with the prototype will help identify any of the user's pain points that you might alleviate in the hack.

Building a quick prototype can be an excellent icebreaker for the team. It can also act as a way to ensure everyone is on the same page, as any ambiguity in the idea will hopefully show itself. A quick prototype is tangible, which will also help your team get behind the concept as up until now, the idea has been only words and rough sketches.

Don't be disheartened if your team doesn't choose your hack idea. Keep it in your back pocket as you might find it's just the thing for a future hack or to build as a side-project.

You should now have found an idea that your whole team can get behind. A hackathon idea acts as the foundation for all future work, so you must get it right. This is a final warning that you should only proceed if you feel as confident as can be that you have appropriately validated and can deliver a product that can present your chosen idea well.

In the next chapter, we will investigate time management. You will be surprised by how fast time will go during a hackathon. Deciding what to prioritise and ordering tasks will be an essential skill to make the most out of your idea.

CHAPTER FIVE

Planning & Timing

Hackathons are monumental challenges with multiple deliverables! More often than not, the deadline is final and late submissions are disqualified. Because of this, being organized and time-efficient is vital. This chapter will first identify how much time each stage of the hackathon process should be allocated to ensure success. We will then deep-dive into the build phase, where we will talk about how you can iterate on your idea to ensure you always have something to show. We'll discuss how to divide up the work and finally examine some methods for keeping the plan on track.

Managing Your Time

As soon as the hackathon starts, most will immediately begin building in a mad frenzy. Don't follow suit. When you reach your desk for the first time, take a moment. Think ahead and split up your time towards all the pieces of your project. Remember you won't be able to use all the time during the event to hack, you still must eat, and it's also a good idea to attend any workshops that are happening. Though how you decide to split your time is up to you, a good example split would look like this:

- **10% Idea Generation:** Time to develop and refine that winning idea! You might use this time to perform the activities outlined in the previous chapter.
- **60% Build:** Time used to turn your idea into a product. Further detail on build planning can be found in the following section.
- **20% Presentation:** Use this time to create the presentation that tells the story of your hackathon journey.
- **5% Submission:** Time dedicated to polishing off any additional documentation required to ensure your product qualifies for the hackathon.
- **5% Team Building:** Time for ceremonies, icebreakers, and any other form of activity that will help you work better as a team.

I suspect some of you may be thinking that that's an awful lot of time dedicated to the presentation. Consider that when you pitch to the judges, your presentation may be on the screen for the same amount of time as your project demo, if not longer! Also, remember that it is not just creating the presentation but also memorizing what you are going to say; every extra second you spend practicing your pitch is an extra ounce of confidence that you will convey.

Though there is a logical step-by-step to each of these stages, you can perform some elements in parallel. For example, during the build phase, you might encounter a complex challenge that you might want to mention in the presentation—adding it immediately to the presentation as soon as its discovered would be ideal as its fresh in your mind. For this reason, it's a good idea to at least have a blank presentation set up as soon as you start so people can jot their thoughts down.

Planning the Build

This book encouraged you to imagine crazy ideas without limitation in the last chapter. As a result, the fantastic idea you have chosen to pursue likely has plenty of additional features that aren't essential. Regardless of the hack's duration, your primary objective for the build phase should be getting to Minimal Viable Prototype (or MVPr for short!).

MVPr

In the context of this book, MVPr is a low fidelity version of your product that you could ask people to try. It has just enough functionality to enable users to perform your hack's function so that you can learn from observing them attempt to complete that task.

When we say "low fidelity", we mean a prototype that does not contain the visual qualities you might see in a final product. You might forgo branding, color, content and even layout. The focus here is entirely on functionality.

You can ensure your planned build is MVPr by using the flow diagram:

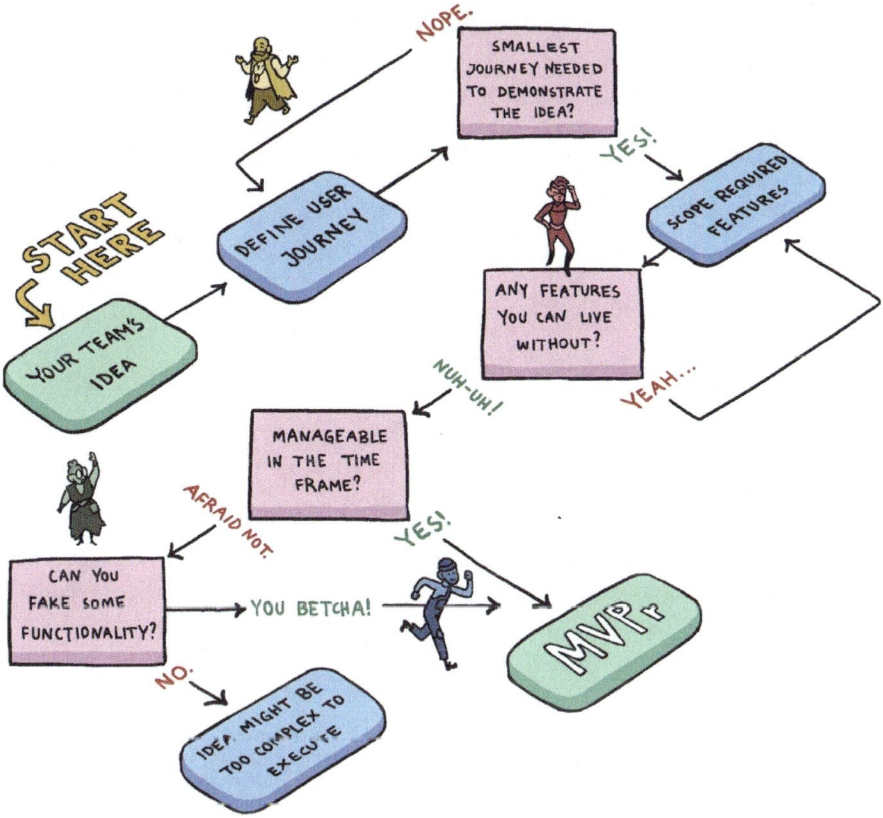

What is considered part of the MVPr (and every future iteration of the product) should be a group decision. Be sure you don't forget any product ideas or features that are cut. Instead, note them down to refer back to later for a future product iteration or for the inevitable question "what else would you do if you had more time?".

By completing your MVPr first, you are guaranteed to have a functioning, demo-able version of your product to show the judges. Sure, it won't look pretty but remember that you've already succeeded if it can convey the idea.

Post-MVPr

After hitting the MVPr milestone, save and commit your work! Have this as a version of your product you can return to and demo if things go wrong. Once you've done that, you have multiple different workstreams open to you. You could:

- Iterate on the MVPr towards Minimal Viable Product (or MVP).
- Enhance the existing MVPr with a visual identity.

The option you choose should be based on remaining time and team ability. Let's look at both of these in more detail.

Iterate Towards MVP

In product development, MVP is a small iteration of your product with just enough features to be usable by early adopters who can then provide feedback. Now is the moment to review the features you cut from the MVPr and add those that will make the product a great experience for users. You should prioritize those low-effort and high-impact features as we can consider these to be "quick wins".

Think smart when you're absorbed by the moment and imagining what your hack could be like if you complete that "one last feature". It's always better to present what you already have with more polish than add a bundle of mediocre additional features.

At this moment, you might also choose to perform other little tasks that make the project accessible to others:

- Attach to a domain: Nothing makes your product look more real than being publicly accessible via the internet.
- Add authentication: If users need to have preferences or data, now is a great time to add authentication so users can have personalized experiences.

Enhance with Visual Identity

At this point, adding a visual identity to the project can be high-impact for those with a team weighting towards front-end and design skills. Some activities you could perform at this moment:

- Use or create a component library so that your site has a consistent feel across the whole user journey.
- Add text to explain to users how to use your product at each stage of the journey.
- Paint the site in color, typography and your logo.

As you can see, branding plays a crucial role in visual identity, that's why Chapter Eight is dedicated to it! I advise checking it out if you are pursuing this avenue.

Post-MVP

In very rare circumstances, when the hackathon duration is months long, you may find you also manage to complete MVP before the deadline. If you find yourself in this fortunate position, the next version of your product you should aim for is a minimal marketable product (MMP). This is the smallest version of the product you could sell. In your presentation, you will want to talk about monetization strategy, but if you can take it one step further and already have your product monetized, you will blow the judges away!

If you're wondering where the planning for the submission and presentation is, don't panic! Chapter Ten and Eleven are dedicated to the submission and presentation, respectively.

Sticking to the Plan

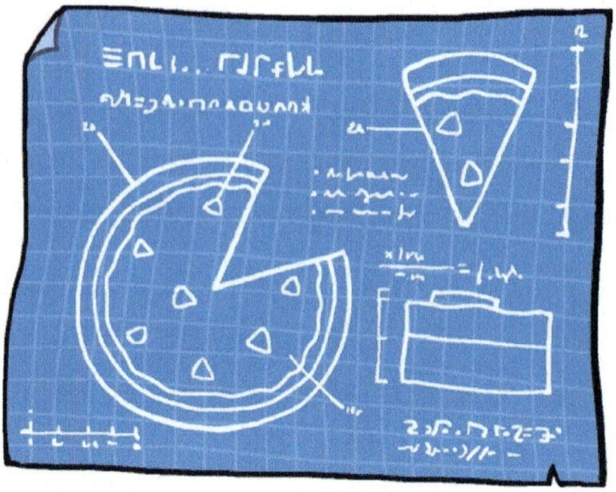

You have a plan of what you want to build and where to spend your time. How do you ensure you're sticking to the plan? When your crew are all working on their individual contributions, you must come back together often. If not, you could have a teammate falling behind without realizing it - a teammate that you could be supporting! A great way to avoid this is to run a couple of mini sessions scattered throughout the hack.

Keep in mind that these sessions can go on for far longer than intended due to their loose structure. Assign a timekeeper who will keep the group on track should you start to stray. Also, assign a shutterbug - any output from these sessions should be captured so that it can be referred back to later. Photos on a half-decent smartphone should do the job.

Ways of Working Session

Suggested Frequency: Once at the beginning of the hackathon.

A "Ways of Working" session is a discussion used to acknowledge that everyone is different. Everyone has different work habits and this meeting acts as an open forum to discuss expectations that we can align on while preserving everyone's ability to focus on their work individually. Hosting this session is critical when you're working with people you've only just met. Understanding how they work best and enabling that will make the team more productive. Keep the session casual.

Here are a few questions you can use to start the session:

- Are you an introvert or an extrovert?
- What is your style of learning? For example visual, audio, kinetic...
- What enables you to be your most productive?
- What are your hopes and fears for the hackathon?
- What do you need from your team members?

If this is the first icebreaker activity your group is doing together, don't be afraid to throw some fun questions in there! E.g. What's your spirit animal? Aside from hackathons, what other hobbies do you have?

When working remote, particularly internationally, also include these questions:

- What time zone are you in?
- What hours will you be working on this project?
- When out of hours, would you rather we don't message you?

Planning Session

Suggested Frequency: Once at the start of each product iteration.

A planning session is a meeting where you decide how to divide and conquer the work. By running this session, you can be sure that you have scoped out the work required to complete each feature and avoid any nasty surprises.

Take the list of features you intend to build and break them down into actionable tasks on post-it notes. You can use different colors to denote what kind of work it is, e.g., blue for front-end and orange for back-end. Be sure to order them so that any dependencies are visible.

You can use these post-it notes to track progress. Leave them on a wall visible to all the team; when a team member is ready to start working, they can take one of the post-its and work on that piece. This avoids two people picking up the same piece of work and gives the whole team an idea of what is remaining to complete.

Celebrating the completion of these tasks is great for morale. Don't let progress go unrecognized!

Scrum Ceremonies

Scrum lends itself to iterative development. While adopting it in its entirety would be overkill for a hackathon, running mini versions of a few scrum ceremonies such as standups and retrospectives can be hugely beneficial.

Standups

Suggested Frequency: Every two hours for short hacks, every day for long hacks.

A standup is a regular meeting that attempts to get teammates on the same page. The aim is to leave knowing whether you are on track or not to deliver what you had set out to do. It also gives people the space to ask for help should they need it.

As the name might suggest, a standup can (and should) be completed standing up. Having these standing up is even more critical in a hackathon environment where you spend most of the day in a sedentary position.

Running a session is as simple as going around the group and getting everyone to answer the following questions:

- What have you been working on?
- What will you work on next?
- Are there any blockers?

Standups are also a great moment to rotate pair programming partners if you are using that technique!

Retrospectives

Suggested Frequency: At the midpoint for short hacks, every three days for long hacks.

A retrospective (retro) is a meeting that creates a moment to pause, reflect on how the team is working, highlight risks and suggest ways to improve future performance. In a hackathon, it is common that your team has only just met. If this is the case, you have no idea how to work with each other yet, and retros can help make the team understand each other and, as a result, move faster.

So how do you run a fun retro? There are many standard templates, but the one that we will focus on is the *Sailboat Retrospective*. To set up the retro, do the following:

1. On a large piece of paper, or a digital board like Miro, draw a sailboat. The sailboat should be on the sea in the middle of the page.
2. In the sky, draw the wind pushing the sailboat from the left. The wind represents the things that are moving us forward towards our goals.
3. In the sky, draw the sun on the right of the sailboard. The sun represents the things that are making us happy.
4. In the water, draw an anchor holding the sailboat down. The anchor represents the things holding us back.
5. Finally, draw a reef underwater to the right. The reef represents anything we would like to call out as an upcoming risk.

Now that you've set this up, give every team member post-it notes (virtual or physical) and ask them to answer the following questions in any order and place them in the relevant section:

- What has propelled us forward so far?
- What are you enjoying?
- What has delayed progress so far?
- Are there any upcoming risks?

If you've done this right, you should have a board that looks something like the following image:

Guide your team through the insights you have uncovered. Acknowledge the good - long may it continue! In the case of upcoming risks and delays, ask, "How can we avoid these?". Any actionable suggestions should be noted down and implemented by the team.

It's best to alternate between the positive and negative sections of the board. If you focus on all the risks or delays first, it can be a little stress-inducing.

Speak up Always

If you are struggling with something, don't wait for a ceremony to raise it. You might find that you have a colleague that in 5 minutes, could fix what might take you 50 minutes of troubleshooting. Vocalizing difficulties can feel unnatural, but a hackathon team is only as strong as the weakest link in the chain. By helping you, the team will be stronger.

For more tips on overcoming challenges that may crop up during a hackathon, browse Chapter Nine - Surviving the Night.

On Track for Greatness!

This chapter has thrown many processes at you. Don't let yourself get bogged down in it. Hackathons can be taken as seriously or casually as you like, so only implement what your team feels they need to work at their best.

You've planned what you want to build, you've got a structure to keep you on track, the only question that remains is "how?". In the next chapter, we will learn all about the various methods you have for implementing the hack depending on your team's ability.

CHAPTER SIX

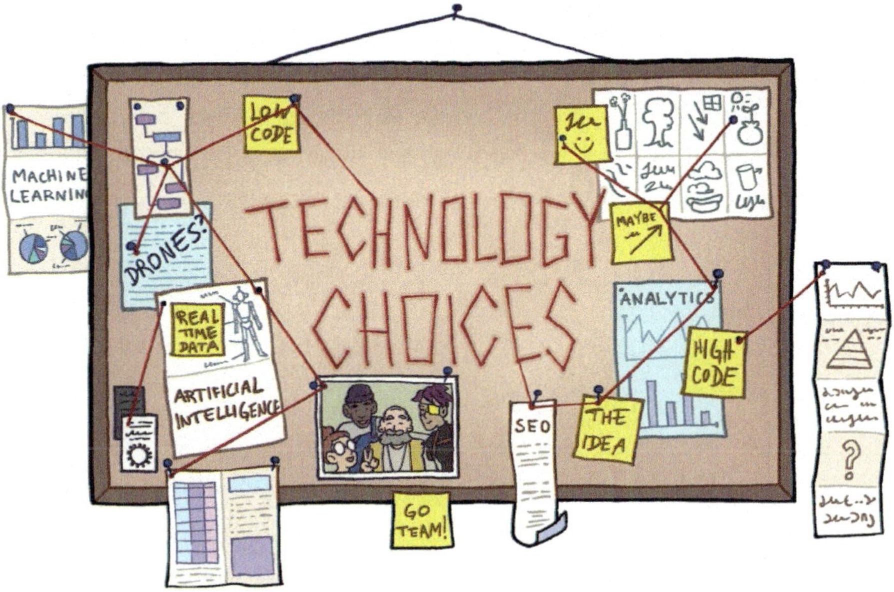

You've decided "what" to build and now want to know "how." Navigating the Wild West of technology with abundant choices can be daunting. In this chapter, we will look at ways in which you can implement your idea and subsequently bring it to life!

When thinking about implementation, your first consideration should always be your teammates. Just because you're a wizard and understand how you might implement the project in one tool or language does not mean it's the correct implementation to enable your team to have the most enjoyable and successful hackathon. You can alienate your teammates if you immediately start building with your toolbox without discussing what your colleagues may want to use. Explore the sections below and discover all the building options your team has before deciding.

There are two main categories of implementation we will be looking at in this chapter - "high-code" and "no-code low-code." Choose based on your team's skill and bravery if the hackathon does not restrict which type you can use. Note that hackathon submission criteria do not always clearly state that you must use high-code. Rules like "must provide complete install and build instructions within the source code repository" would indicate that you should use high-code. A rule like "must provide a working demo" is more open to interpretation, and low-code no-code may be a possibility. Once again, this is a reminder to read the rules thoroughly! Let's start by investigating high-code.

High-code

High-code is the classical method for software assembly - using code! Code and experience are tightly coupled, and as a result, the interface is controlled entirely by developers. From this description, you would be right in thinking that they are highly reliant on your developers. If your team is light on developers, it may be better to take the low-code approach.

You may already be proficient in one or more programming languages, but at any hackathon, you'll always have the choice between something you know and learning something new. It is always tempting to stick to what you know to appear confident, especially among your peers. Remember that hackathons are specifically set up as environments to help you try something new! However, if you haven't coded before, there is no better place to start!

Suggestions for Coding Newbies

One Language to Rule them All.

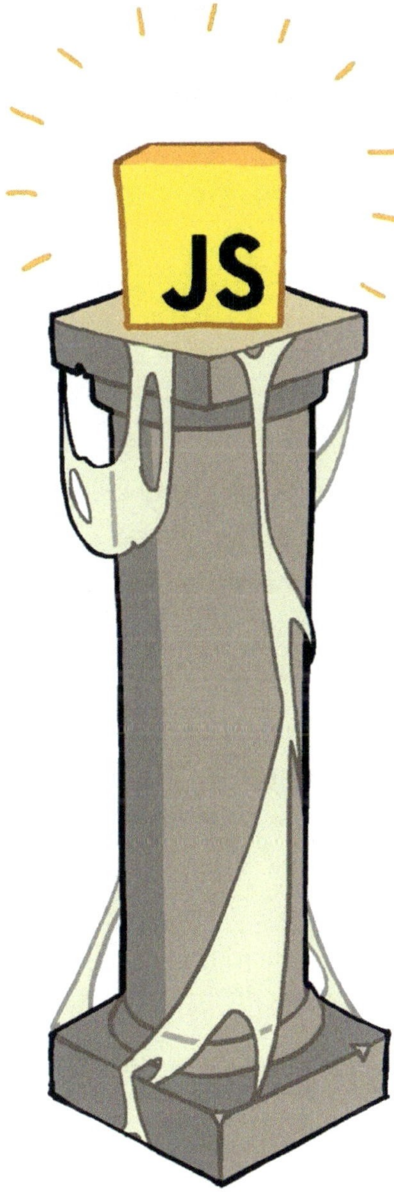

If your team is new to both front-end and back-end development, Javascript might be a great language for the whole team to learn. It is a very versatile language that can be used for both APIs and UIs. If you opt for JavaScript, all developers in the team can help debug issues, regardless of where in the stack the issues occur.

Draw It All Out.

Draw out your project's architecture, data structures, and schema beforehand, especially if you're passing around data between a front-end and back-end. Working out how it will look first will save time when implementing it and help your whole team get on the same page.

Code Formatting.

Use a linter to format your code. A linter is a static code analysis tool used to find programming mistakes, bugs, stylistic blunders, and questionable constructs. Using a linter will make your code easier to read by other developers as its style will be consistent.

The Barrier To Front-End Libraries Is Lower Than You Think

If you already understand the structure of HTML, UI libraries such as ReactJS would not be a significant step up in complexity as the JSX file type is syntactically similar. Before you dive into HTML, consider if there is a technology that might build on that knowledge instead.

Use Version Control

Version control is the practice of tracking and handling changes to code. Simply put, it's a system of record that can tell you how code was changed, when, and by whom.

This is a hack; I don't need version control. Right? Wrong! Using version control might seem like it will slow down your progress, but committing regularly will allow you to time travel. Why is this a good thing? Well, let's say you try to implement just one more feature before the end of the hack, but you end up breaking your codebase; you can quickly jump back to when everything was working to show the judges. Magic.

There is no question which is the world's most popular version control system - git! Although GIT is sometimes referred to as Global Information Tracker, its creator (Linus Torvalds) confirmed that git is named after the word "git" which, in British English slang, means a stupid or unpleasant person.

We won't cover how to use git in this book- there are plenty of results on Google for that. Git is a big beast, however, so let's quickly identify which operations you might want to understand specifically for a hackathon setting:

- Installing git
- Creating repositories
- Creating branches
- Committing code

- Pull requests
- Handling merge conflicts

Don't treat version control as an afterthought - it is a common mistake just to push all the code into GitHub (or equivalent) and merge everything when the project is in its finished state at the end of the hack. This isn't good for two reasons. First, you're probably going to encounter a few merge conflicts with little time to remedy them. Second, judges like to see the evolution of the project - one huge commit does not give them great insight into how it was built over time.

If you're nervous about using git via the terminal, there are some great apps to help make it simpler! I would suggest Googling "GitHub Desktop"!

I JUST CAN'T FIND THE BUG IN MY JS CODE.
WHEN IN DOUBT, CONSOLE.LOG IT OUT.

No-code / Low-code

As the name suggests, No-code / Low-code is an assembly method that requires little to no coding experience. Instead, these platforms use drag-and-drop functionality and visual guidance to help you create your project. It means that anybody in your team, regardless of their technical abilities or expertise, will be able to work on the project. This is an excellent option for those teams with few-to-no developers who would rather spend their time designing and managing information.

This is crazy, right? Building software without code might sound alien, but it's here to stay. In the future, all professional software developers may use low-code solutions to build out the repetitive pieces of code to allow them to focus on the more complex parts of functionality.

Upon hearing about this technology, your immediate question is probably, "is hand-coding your application better?" and the answer is it depends on the scenario. Judges tend to look more favorably on solutions that are coded by hand, so keep that in consideration. But if you haven't got the dev-power to make a fully-fledged MVP, this might be a great alternative.

There are some disadvantages associated with No-code / Low-code you should be aware of:

- **Customization Restriction:** The style, animation, look, and feel of your site are restricted to what the platform vendor provides. This can limit your ability to show your creativity.
- **Cost & Subscription**: Typically, No Code / Low Coder platforms charge a monthly subscription fee. This fee is likely to be higher than self-hosting a coded project. You'll need to remember to cancel the subscription at the end of the hackathon too!
- **Vendor Lock-in:** If you build your MVP within one platform, it can be challenging to move it. This is something you need to consider in cases when you think you will work on and expand the hackathon project after the hackathon is over.

Quick Tip! No-code / Low-code is also an excellent method for creating an MVPr (a concept explored in the previous chapter). As there is no barrier to entry, everyone can help contribute to the prototype, leading to quicker prototype production and product evolution.

No-Code/Low-Code Platforms

If you are interested in pursuing a no-code/low-code implementation, here are some recommendations to get you started.

For Website Development:

WebFlow

Website: **https://webflow.com**

WebFlow is an in-browser design tool that gives you the ability to build and launch responsive websites visually without writing a line of code. 0.5% of all websites use WebFlow so they must be doing something right. That might not sound like a huge number, but that's hundreds of thousands of sites with millions of visitors.

WebFlow is the best option for those that want total control. You might start the project as No-code, but you can quickly start adding your code to the platform when you want to expand the product. They also offer a complimentary content management system without storage limits.

Editor X

Website: **https://www.editorx.com**

Editor X is WebFlow's main competitor, providing much of the same functionality. One advantage that Editor X has over WebFlow is that it can support multiple people editing the same website at the same time. Editor X is also better choice for online stores because it offers more affordable e-commerce plans and can support subscriptions and memberships.

For Mobile App Development:

Bravo

Website: **https://www.bravostudio.app**

Bravo allows you to design your app in Figma or Adobe XD, you can then connect it to any APIs you like. For example you could hook it up to Airtable to create a basic database. Once you're happy, Bravo will then convert the project into a complete mobile application that you can submit to the App Store or Google Play Store.

Play

Website: **https://www.createwithplay.com**

Play is a mobile application that helps you build complete mobile applications without ever leaving your phone. Creating the app experience is all completed via swipes and taps in their easy-to-use UI. Due to the project being siloed to your phone, this tool is not great for collaboration. However, it might be a quick way to set up a companion app for your main project?

Bonus Tools:

Notion

Website: **https://www.notion.so**

While Notion cannot be used to create full software products, it still deserves an honorable mention! Within Notion, you can create databases that are interactive(like an excel spreadsheet). This makes them very easy to edit and manage. If you want a cheap alternative to a Content Management System, this might work for you.

Anima

Website: **https://www.animaapp.com**

Anima is a tool that takes design files from Figma, Sketch, or Adobe XD and converts them into HTML, React, or Vue code. If your team only wants to do a little code, this is a great way to free up your time so that you only need to focus on the core functionality.

General Implementation Tips

The majority of time in a hackathon is dedicated to implementation. Being savvy and smart with how you use this time is essential. Here are some quick tips that may give you the edge:

Fake It Till You Make It

Fake it if time is pressing. The chances are that the judges won't have enough time to delve deep into your project and be sure it's all working as you say it is under the hood. If you are stuck on something for a long time, find a way to fake the functionality. Your idea is more important than your code.

Important Note! Sometimes "implementation" is part of the judging criteria. If this is the case, you should not fake the core functionality of the application. It's also critical in this case to document and submit any dummy functionality to ensure you don't misrepresent your achievements.

Split Into Sub Teams

If most of your team is primarily suited towards a low code solution, but one or more team members want to code, you can split into two sub-teams and have the coders demonstrate part of the solution in code. Splitting can be a smart way to go as it shows that you recognize that the time didn't allow you to show it all in code, and you created a balance of both options instead.

Note Extra Avenues

Idea generation doesn't stop just because you have decided what to build. Your brain will continue to fire new ideas, extra features and different directions for the project. You probably won't have the time to implement all of them, but don't dismiss these sparks of brilliance! Note them all down.

One great thing to cover during the presentation of your project is the "next steps", and having a list of the next handful of elements you want to add to your project demonstrates that the project is more than just a "hack" but a product with a future.

For example, maybe you are building an API that you want to be consumable by your website or app. During development, you ask yourself if there is any benefit to having it publicly accessible. This could be a great monetization strategy as you might charge for access creating a consistent stream of revenue. But you're short on time, and working out how to generate and distribute API keys might be beyond the scope of the project. Instead, you could talk about it in your presentation and demonstrate that you are thinking ahead.

Construction Underway!

You're now in my favorite part of the hack, where you are in total control. Stay focused, keep your team motivated, and soon, that idea will be a lot more than just a concept. In the frenzy of the build, it can feel quite manic but always take a moment to enjoy the speed at which you're building - you don't get this at a day job!

In the next chapter, we will learn how to quickly surround your product with a brand that will stand out.

CHAPTER SEVEN

UX WINS

As discussed in Chapter Three, UX design is the process of creating products that provide meaningful and personally relevant experiences. You can dedicate hours and hours to meticulously analyzing every step of the user experience, but you don't have time for this. So instead, we will focus on a few key areas that, if considered, will elevate your hack with minimal effort.

This chapter features some of the least appealing pizza slices you have ever seen. If you ever see pizza of this color in your local vicinity, best not to eat it.

Create With Your Users in Mind

While building your product, you must keep your users at the front of your mind to ensure that you don't move in a direction that might hinder their experience. Remember that you are not your users, and what you think is right might not correlate with how users find it. It is never a waste of time to pause development and test what you have created with a random hackathon-goer. Sit them down with your app and ask them to talk aloud about their experience using it. Listen for pain points you might want to alleviate.

I guarantee that small sporadic tests like this will provide you with more information than attempting to guess what your users want. They will uncover things you hadn't even thought about!

Design Inspiration

Jakob's Law tells us that users spend most of their time on other sites. This means that users prefer your site to work the same way as other sites they already know. If you ever needed permission to copy or get inspired by what is already there, this is it! While working on a feature, ask yourself, "Have I seen this implemented well before?". If your answer is "Yes!" go and revisit that app or webpage where you experienced it. Soak up as much information as you can about what makes the experience great, and then "port" it to your hack.

Be open about what has inspired design decisions. You may consider it as cheating if you're new to this, but copying flows and layouts is widespread within the industry. Why should you waste time and money researching the best way to create a login screen when hundreds of other companies have already perfected this? One smart way to phrase it might be - "we identified that X worked well in the industry and decided a similar pattern would work well within our use case." This shows an awareness of the market that you might not otherwise be able to demonstrate.

Color

Working with color is 50% art and 50% science, and if you don't know what you're doing, 100% frustrating! This section will talk about making better color choices within your apps and websites.

Before we jump into this section, remember that while color choices are important, *remaining true to your project's personality is paramount.* If the following information has you thinking that you should change from "that wacky pink and yellow combo," but you'll lose some "wackiness," then I would vote to keep it.

Color Psychology

If you think of the color red and where you see it in your daily life, you probably will associate it with words like "stop," "cancel," "warning," or "danger." If you did, you're not alone! Colors subconsciously communicate emotion to us all, every moment of every day. Most people have the same pool of emotions invoked by the same color in Western world, though it can vary between cultures. It's essential to understand what common emotions are invoked so that you can make better choices for the colors you use. Let's look at a collection of colors now and their effect on your audience.

Status Colors

When choosing colors to indicate statuses, evaluate the below - don't label confirmation buttons red and cancel buttons green! It's a common mistake that can be easily avoided with just a moment's thought.

- **Red:** Communicates caution, danger, and warnings. While it is most known for being associated with hazards, it can also be linked to action, excitement, and passion. Use for attracting attention to your application! Avoid using it as your primary color as you don't want users having their warning bells going as soon as they land on your site.

- **Orange:** Communicates warmth, optimism, and adventure. Great for indicating that something is still in progress.

- **Yellow:** Communicates positivity and opportunity. Like orange, it's great for indicating that something is still in progress. Use in moderation as too much can induce anxiety.

- **Green:** Communicates harmony, growth, nature, and reliability. Use for confirmations and submit actions.

Neutral Colors

- **Black:** Communicates sophistication. Black adds high contrast to a palette and is helpful for text color in the cooperation of light backgrounds to improve copy legibility.
- **White:** Communicates purity. Great for keeping things simple but be careful of using too much as it can create the feeling of loneliness.

When working with black and white, reduce eye strain by avoiding using the blackest black on the whitest white!

Brand colors

- **Pink:** Communicates calm love, kindness, and femininity. Fun fact pre-20th century, pink was considered a masculine color. Pink is often seen in the brands of fashion, beauty industries and non-profits.
- **Purple:** Communicates wisdom, creativity, and power. It is associated with entertainment and religion.
- **Blue:** Communicates order, trust, honesty, and loyalty. Banks and social media platforms commonly use blue to inspire dependability.
- **Gold:** Communicates wealth and success. Standard in the fashion and beauty industries. Use tastefully, as too much gold can make your product look egotistical.

If you're looking for a site to use as an example of 'good use of color' check out GitHub.com!

A Whistle-Stop Tour of Color Theory

Color Harmonies

Color harmonies are all science-backed methods for pairing colors together in aesthetically pleasing ways using geometry. If you've heard the terms "monochromatic," "complementary," or "analogous," - then you likely already know what some harmonies look like without even realizing it. All harmonies are found by combining shapes such as squares and triangles with the color wheel. Let's look at some examples:

When attempting to find colors that complement your primary color choice, consider these harmonies to try and find a combination that users will find pleasing to the eye. Set one of the corners of these shapes to your primary color, sit back, and let the edges of the shape point you in the right direction of what to pair with your primary color.

Remember that it's okay to play with the saturation of these colors! If all your colors are of equal brightness, they will all punch less.

SIMILAR SATURATION AND BRIGHTNESS — VARYING LEVELS OF SATURATION AND BRIGHTNESS

Coolors

(https://coolors.co)

If you would rather not do all the geometry yourself, Coolors is a great website that can create color themes for you. Once you load up the generator, you can hit the space bar until you find a palette you're happy with, then copy the color hex codes. If you already have one or two colors in mind, you can paste in your hex values and lock them in place so that the generator only finds colors that will work with your choices.

Pro Tip! If you want to specify which color harmony method you want the generator to use precisely, you can find it hidden in the settings menu - the option you're looking for is called "Generate Method." They have options for all of the harmonies mentioned above and more!

Neutral Colors

Neutral colors are like the groupies for your primary color. They can be warm, cool, light, or dark, but they aim to recede into the background leaving room for your primary color to work its magic. The most common neutral colors are blacks, whites, grays, and browns. They can also be very light or very dark variants of your primary color - these are known as "near neutrals"!

Neutral colors are best used for areas where you don't want your users to pay attention. For example, you might use a neutral gray for the background of your website or app, where you would rather the user pay attention to the form in front. Neutrals are also useful for creating visual effects - you can use darker and lighter tones to create a shadow effect or similar lighting effect.

Limit Your Palette

The more bright colors you use, the less any individual color will stand out. If you want to direct your user's attention to one specific task, ensure that color is used explicitly to make it stand out. You can stick to neutral colors except for your site logo and calls to action.

Beware of Contrast

The colors you use for your background and foreground elements must create an appropriate contrast to make your application legible to all people. There are an estimated 285+ million people in the world living with a visual impairment. This is a large number of people to be excluded just because of your color choices.

An excellent resource for checking your design's contrast is the web aim contrast checker (https://webaim.org/resources/contrastchecker). Simply enter your color hex codes and cross your fingers - if your site passes, you can breathe a sigh of relief. If, however, they don't pass, then don't panic! Use the slider to try and find a combination of your colors that would make your site more accessible.

Contrast is just the tip of the iceberg for improving websites and apps for the visually impaired, but it's a great place to start.

Notes on Typography

Your typography style is not just about making your hack look cool - typography is a communication device between you and your users. It must remain clear whenever you are providing the user with instructions or essential information. Here are some quick tips that should work in any layout design:

- **Keep things simple:** If you're not used to working with lots of different fonts - don't! A hackathon project can be completed with a single font. By sticking to one, you remove the stress of finding font pairings that work. You'll also master it quicker, giving you more time to focus on other elements.
- **When in doubt, justify left:** In western culture, we are used to reading text left to right. Justifying your text to the left makes it easier for users to find the start of paragraphs. It also stops their eyes from zigzagging when moving between centered texts of different lengths.
- **Emphasizing weight:** When you want to make something pop and are considering using bold or extra bold, make sure it is two weights above your average weight. If you jump a single weight, the weight difference might not be as noticeable to the user.
- **Double for Titles:** A great little trick to make your titles and headings stand out is to double the pixels! If you use 16px for your body text, double this to 32px for your headings.

Create Delight

When taking users on a journey through your project, try and induce happy emotions. After all, you want them to come out of it having had a positive experience. It doesn't take a lot to make flows more gracious; a simple animation, emoji, or celebratory image can cheer up a journey.

I think it's our duty to make our users smile. Reward them. As a user I am always hoping you will give me a virtual high-five when I do something you and I agree is awesome.

Keep It Simple

Clutter is your number one enemy. If users have to climb obstacles or hunt around to achieve their goal, they will get infuriated. If there are elements that don't need to be there, ask yourself if they should be there. As a general rule, fewer distractions mean faster user task speed. Please keep it clean and simple.

This also applies to the text within your product. Be concise with your words when conveying critical information. Fewer words will help users understand your intent faster. If you increase the amount of text users have to read, you will see users skim-read the copy, which may lead to them misunderstanding it.

Keep It Consistent

Keep design consistent across pages so users can easily work out that they are on the same site. As web users, we are all constantly redirected or navigated away from the website page we are visiting. This happens so fast these days that it's sometimes difficult to be sure whether we are still on the same site or not. By giving your site a consistent feel using color and labeling, users can be reassured that they are where they thought they were.

Consistency can also extend beyond design. It would help if you took care to ensure that your site's functionality behaves consistently as well so that users can learn to navigate your site efficiently. As an example, clicking on a hyperlink should always open the link in a new tab within the browser (though this is not a general rule).

UX-y is the New Sexy

Armed with your new-found user experience powers, you should be ready to design in a user-centered way to create experiences that your users will love - no matter who they are!

In the next chapter, we are going to talk about branding. We will be using branding to give your hackathon project its sense of identity. Color shows up there too, so be sure to bring the knowledge from this chapter into that section

CHAPTER EIGHT

"Branding" refers to the elements of your product that give it a sense of identity. They make it easy distinguish your product or company from someone else's. This chapter will focus on four main branding elements - the product's name, brand colors, logo, and copywriting that we can use to give your product a brand boost at speed.

Quick reminder! As the title of this chapter suggests, this chapter focuses on getting your hack an identity in minimal time. It is by no means a comprehensive guide to branding. Companies spend hundreds of hours and piles of money to make decisions that we will make in five minutes. However, all of the elements in the chapter should work together to fulfill the five-second rule.

The Five-Second rule

When a judge is presented with your project, they should be able to understand what it does within five seconds of seeing it. Why five seconds? Because this is the average time it will take them to form their first impression. If they don't understand or like what they see, they are less likely to want to engage with your product. It's also vital that there is a clear call to action to show users where they can start the journey you want to take them on.

Naming Your Hack

The name of your hackathon project will most likely be the word seen the most throughout your application and uttered during your talk - you better make sure it's the right one! Some quick tips for naming a hackathon are as follows:

- **Keep It Short and Memorable**: The shorter the better. The judges are going to see plenty of hacks. Is your hack's name memorable enough to stand out from the rest? *Less than ten characters is my rule!*
- **Choose A Name That Is Searchable:** Will a search for the product name on Google lead me to your product, or does it share its name with a million other products and services that may be ranked higher?
- **Avoid Spelling Ambiguity:** Make sure the name of your project is not difficult to spell. Also, avoid using words that are homophones. Homophones are words that sound the same but

have different spelling and meanings. E.g., the words "flower" and "flour."

- **Align It with a Domain:** Make sure the domain for your chosen name is available. Buy it early. Getting the domain name activated can take a long time, and if you leave it until the final stretch, you'll be too late to get anything deployed to the site.
- **Waste No More Time on It:** The name is not important - the idea is. It's important to dedicate time this, but you also have to know when to stop. If you've spent more than twenty minutes on the name, you're doing something wrong.

Brand Colors

As discussed in the previous chapter, people associate different colors with different meanings. Induce the right emotion in your users by using appropriate colors. Be sure to reread the section on color psychology before making a definitive choice.

Another great little tip is to use the color spectrum to find a gap for your brand. First, collect the brand colors associated with your competitors, then plot them on a visible light spectrum. When you've finished, look for an area with few competitors and use a color found within it for your brand. Consumers will be unlikely to associate your brand with your competitors if it is radically different from them.

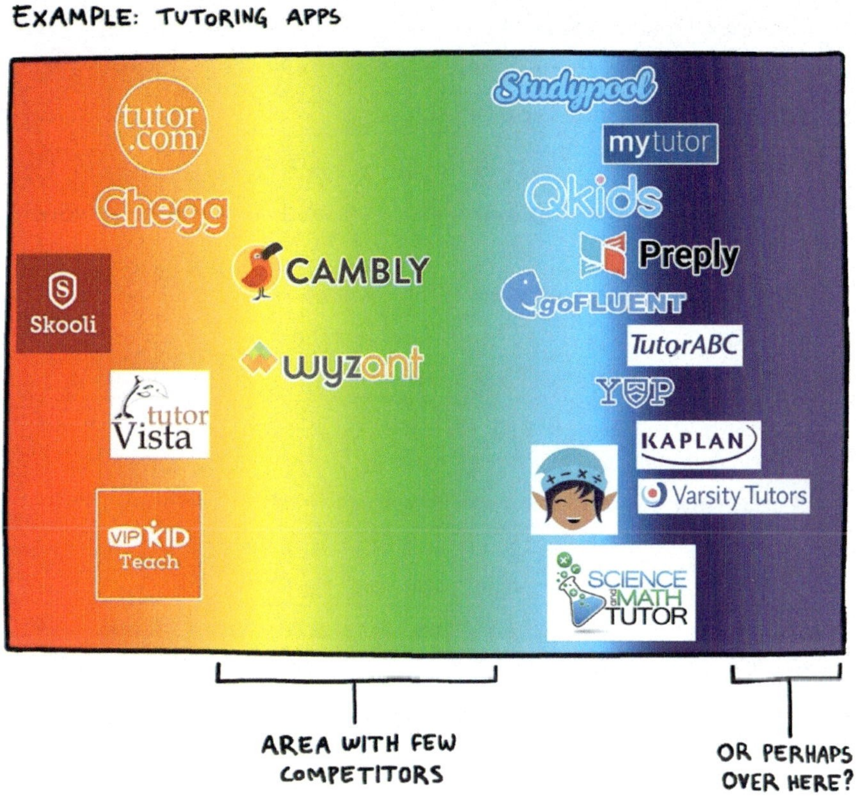

Don't forget that if your app sits inside something larger, e.g. it behaves like a third-party integration or chrome extension for a specific site, make sure that your brand colors do not clash with the parent application.

Your Logo

A brand logo is a symbol that can represent your company, team or (in our case) product! Don't misinterpret that - the logo is just the face of your brand, a minimal representation. It doesn't have to embody *all* of your product features in one design.

Logos are the asset most often reshaped, recolored, and used externally. As a result, they need to be the most versatile of all your assets. Keep these questions in your mind while you create yours:

- **Does your logo match your name?** Your name should complement your logo and vice versa. Ensure the two work together.
- **Are you settling too soon?** Don't settle on the first logo design you're happy with. The chances are that there is another great one just around the corner! Logos are something you might want to sketch sporadically throughout the hackathon while you let your subconscious work on other problems.
- **Does your logo work both big and small?** Your logo will be seen everywhere, from the favicon in your browser tab (16x16px) to full screen on a presentation slide (~1500x1500px). While designing, ensure that it works at these two extremes and everywhere in between.
- **Does your logo work monochromatically?** Your logo will probably be placed on multiple different backgrounds during the hack: within your app or website, readme, presentation, and submission material. It might also be printed in black and white at some point. So, be sure that your logo works when converted to a monochromatic color theme. One great way to improve the monochromatic appearance of your logo is to convert your colors to HSL(hue, saturation, and lightness) values and then manipulate their light values.
- **Are you making use of negative space?** The negative space (the areas without any color) is as important as the positive space. Try to be consistent with your use of negative space, keeping it even and geometric.

Copywriting Tips

If you're looking for some small tweaks you can make to help you connect more powerfully with your users, this is the section for you! How your app conveys information and its tone will impact how users feel about your brand. Your copy needs to do three things: build trust, show authority and offer the next steps. You can cover these bases by ensuring your project answers the following five questions:

- **What can your product do for me?**
- **Why should I listen to you?**
- **What makes your product different?**
- **What makes you legit?**
- **Where do I start?**
- **Why should I stick around?**

One great way to think about all these questions is by using the spotlight method.

The Spotlight Method

In business, the spotlight can either be on you or your customers. If the spotlight is on you, the focus of your copy is likely on your passion and your goals. However, when you shift that spotlight over to your users, the focus is on their problems, aspirations, and goals. Unfortunately, most of us get this wrong in our writing. Generally speaking, we shine way too much of that spotlight on ourselves and not our users. Again, you are not your users. Customers want to feel heard and acknowledged, so make sure that the spotlight is on them when you're writing text. Let's look at a specific example.

Let's pretend you've created an app that allows people to perform a self-service checkout at a supermarket. The headline of your website says the following: "Your all-in-one solution to supermarket self-checkout." From a spotlight perspective, there's a problem here as there is no benefit or hook for the client who is likely on the site as they want to check out faster. This copy is about the product, not the customer. Of course, it is obvious to users that self-checkout is faster, but it would be better if users didn't have to decode this. Using the spotlight method we could transform this headline into "Making your checkout experience 250% faster." This shifts the focus to how the product is solving the nuisance of slow checkouts.

Consistency is Key

Everything that we have mentioned in these sections has been focused on your hack, but it's important to remember that your brand extends beyond the code - It's highly beneficial to ensure that your presentation and submission adhere to the brand guidelines you've defined here.

You now have all the ways of working, processes, design, and implementation considerations to go away and build your prototype. Before you do, though, read the next chapter. The build is arguably the most prolonged and intense part of the process. So, let's pause and switch the focus to you - your mental and physical health.

CHAPTER NINE

SURVIVING THE NIGHT

Hackathons will test you both physically and mentally. This chapter makes that burden a little easier by providing you with some preparation ideas and remediation techniques. We'll first talk about what you should take to the event. We'll then investigate project pitfalls and how to avoid or mend them. Finally, we will talk about staying healthy regardless of hackathon duration.

The Kit List

I have turned up to a hackathon many a time and found myself missing something that could have been useful. I want to stop you from ending up in this situation. This is everything I would take to a hackathon:

Smartphone: You'll network with many people at the event. Having LinkedIn installed will make it easier to contact them after the event.

Display Adapters: Don't assume the organizers have all the peripherals you might need during your presentation. Make sure you have an adapter that allows your laptop to output via HDMI.

An Extra Jumper: In-person hackathons often need large venues. Venues that might not have a whole lot of heating. There's nothing worse than feeling cold and tired so make sure you keep warm!

Laptop: Duh!

Chargers: This might seem like common sense, but turning up to a hackathon without a laptop or phone charger is common!

A Water Bottle: As we will discuss in this chapter. Water is essential, so make sure you have a vessel to carry it!

A Pillow: A pillow is to hackathons what a towel is to *The Hitchhiker's Guide to the Galaxy*. If you stay at the hackathon overnight, you might fancy a quick nap to recharge your batteries. A pillow will help you sleep as comfortably as possible. It can also double up as a cushion to make that chair remain comfortable after sitting for an extended period!

If you're looking to make friends, bring a few spares of some of the kit list. You'll find that others won't be as prepared as you are, and handing someone your spare phone charger can be a great conversation starter.

Common Project Pitfalls & Remedies

While I hope that your hackathon is a positive experience, sometimes, things can go wrong. Knowing how to handle issues can help you move on from them faster.

If you are attending your first hackathon, this section is crucial. Newbie! Try not to let one challenging moment taint your hackathon experience. When something negative does happen, it's easy to let that take all of your focus. As it does, you can let that negativity consume you, or you can consciously decide to try and "turn it around." Your attitude will directly affect how quickly and effectively you can turn the tide. Be the example. Be the helpful, organized one who makes things better for everyone.

And if you genuinely are not able to complete the hackathon as a result of one of these pitfalls, try and remember that it's not a reflection on hackathons as a whole. I assure you that if you try again, you'll come to love the format.

Lack of Motivation

Humans naturally like to take the easy route. Anything challenging requires motivation to get us there. Hackathons are no exception. As events that test you both mentally and physically, it's crucial that you and your team feel motivated.

Celebrate the Little Things

A straightforward way to keep motivation up is to celebrate the little things! Made a tricky design decision as a team? Did you work out how all the puzzle pieces will combine? Got your front-end and back-end talking to each other? These all sound like high-five worthy moments.

One of the best mini celebrations I've experienced was at around 10.45 PM after 3 hours of debugging. We had finally fixed a pesky piece of code and realized that the pub would still be open. We left the hackathon venue and got a round of celebratory drinks in just before the "last call" bell rang! Felt like fate!

Get to Know Each Other

People are more likely to be motivated if they are invested in the people they work with. If you and your teammates don't know each other prior to the hack, encourage the group to participate in activities together. You could suggest that you all grab a coffee together from that place around the corner. Or set up some healthy rivalries with neighboring teams in a ping-pong championship (loser buys the previously mentioned coffee!)

Losing a Teammate

You might find that a teammate is not as invested as you in the project you are working on. They might not believe in the idea or feel like they are not contributing a considerable amount to the project. If you start to recognize these feelings in a teammate, first attempt to raise motivation using the techniques in the previous section. However, sometimes it is simply not possible to rouse them, and if you can't, the most probable outcome is that they leave halfway through project development. This typically happens in one of two ways - they vocalize it or vanish.

If they've vanished, the first thing to check is whether they have really left the project. Are you sure they have not just stepped out for a break? Try to contact the individual calmly and politely - being frantic won't help them feel like coming back! Hopefully, you hear from them, but assume the worst if it's been an hour and you don't hear anything. Hackathons are time-sensitive, so wasting precious time chasing someone for longer can be a poor use of time.

Now that we are sure that the individual has left the team, it's vital to assess their role and contribution. Ask yourself the big question: **Can the team finish the project without this person?** If you can, fantastic! If your team can complete the project with the remaining members and technical know how, it's best just to continue. Introducing the hack idea to someone and getting them set up on the project is probably not worth your time. If, however, you feel you couldn't finish the project, then you have a couple of options:

- **Join Forces:** It's unlikely that you are the only team that has seen people leave during the event. If you can find another group in the same situation as you, you might decide to join together to form a new team. If your ideas are compatible, you might combine them into one super-project, or you may choose one of the two ideas to pursue.

- **Find a Late Participant:** If the departure happens early on in the hack, you might find that a participant who arrives late might be your saving grace! If you can find the skills you are looking for in someone who arrives late, encourage them to join your project. They are also likely to be enthusiastic as they might struggle to find a team when the hack is already underway.
- **Ask for Mentor Support:** Mentors are there to support you with situations exactly like this. Mentors can help you find solutions to technical problems, or they might even write some code for you!
- **Upskill Yourself:** There's never a better time to learn something new than right now. If you feel a little light on work, perhaps you might volunteer to cover the missing piece and be the real hero?

Don't lose hope if you cannot get any of the above to work; hackathons are about presenting ideas, not finished, deployed, technical products! If you can still present your idea well, you can still come out of it with victory! More on this in the next chapter!

Technical Struggles

Issues that pop up aren't always centered around people. Teams can also struggle with a myriad of technically related issues. It's important to remember that judges are never expecting miracles. Failure to implement all technical details is not the same as failing the hackathon. While you absolutely should try and work through them, some problems demand more time than you have available. That's why it's important to...

Timebox Problem Solving

It's always a good idea to try and solve problems yourself before looking further afield. But, regardless of what trouble you are trying to solve, you are always working against the clock. Timebox your time for finding a solution. Give yourself thirty minutes to work it out and if you still haven't found the answer, continue with the ideas in the sections below.

Technically Too Complex

No matter how well you plan, sometimes technical complexities won't show up until you are 12 hours into coding your project. When these complexities arise, your team might realize that the challenge you have undertaken is not feasible within the time frame. In this situation, you have three possible routes:

- **Simplify:** Can the functionality be simplified?
- **Backtrack:** Would building this functionality be more straightforward to create in another coding language or format?
- **Fake It:** Could you fake this functionality to better demonstrate the idea? This is a last resort only.

Language Nuances

Hackathons are safe spaces to learn something new, and you are often encouraged to learn new programming languages. Learning isn't instant, no matter how much of a "sponge" you are. If you are working with a language for the first time and are struggling to find the correct syntax, consider these tips (listed in the order you should approach them):

- **Perform a Google Search:** Sometimes, the answer is a Google search away! If you already know the syntactical vocabulary from another programming language, try combining that with the language you are trying to implement. For example "for loop JavaScript" - A for loop is something that exists in most programming languages under the sun. Combining this search with the language you're working in will lead to example code you may be able to use.

- **Search the GitHub Universe:** GitHub is the most prominent source code host on the internet. With hundreds of millions of code repositories publicly accessible, searching the platform can be a great way to find code implementations similar to your own.
- **Ask a Mentor:** Call upon one of the individuals specifically there to help! When engaging with a mentor, get to your answer quicker by first explaining what the problem is and how you have already tried to fix it. This stops them from repeating ideas you have already tried.
- **Announce it to the Room/Social Channel:** It's sometimes easy to forget that many technical people surround you. If a mentor can't help you, it might be the case that another participant at the event can. There is no harm in throwing the question out to the room. That one embarrassing moment for you might save you hours of searching.

Struggling with a Bug

The code doesn't always misbehave just because of your lack of understanding. You might have the syntax perfect and still have errors. Here are some ways to find the answers:

- **Paste into Google:** If your code is erroring out, the simplest remediation is often just to copy and paste the error into Google.
- **Stack Overflow:** Ask the world's biggest question and answer forum for programmers! But before asking your question, check that there isn't already a similar question published on the platform that might have the answers you need.
- **Ask a Mentor:** In exactly the same way as the previous section!

Can't Tie It All Together

One of the most frustrating things is when you have the front-end and back-end working independently until the final few hours. If this is the case, there is often a frantic rush to join them together, and you might find that sometimes the jigsaw pieces just don't fit. This can be because the plan for how the parts will work together was miscommunicated early on, or perhaps one part is not quite finished.

In either case, communication upfront is the best possible path to remediation. If you get close to time and don't think you will be able to glue the two pieces together, don't panic! There is no harm in showing these pieces in your demo separately while explaining how they will work together in the future.

Capture These Experiences!

Hindsight is a beautiful thing. You'll probably look back on these difficulties and think you could have handled them better. Instead of keeping this to yourself, talk about it in your submission and presentation. This shows a great deal of transparency and shows how human you are to the judges, which is never a bad thing!

Staying Healthy

While the hack is underway, it's essential to look after your body and mind. There is a direct correlation between your health and the quality of your work. The points you'll want to keep in mind vary depending on hackathon duration, so let's investigate a few different lengths.

One Day Hackathons

Get Up and Walkaround!

When time is limited, it's easy to stay glued to your seat but try and stand up and walk around at least once per hour. Say hi to another hackathon team (and get a sneak peek at the competition!) or breathe some fresh air. If you are struggling with something, this is even more important - give your subconscious the space to work the problem.

Support

Being mindful and supporting each other is more important in shorter hacks as you have less time to ideate and build. When you have a problem, voice it. If no one in your team is aware that you're struggling, they can't help. If a team member expresses a concern, try to huddle around it and find a solution as quickly as possible. You'll be quicker as a group.

Weekend Hackathons

Regular Check-Ins

Check-in with your teammates every few hours, whether working remote or in person. Each team member has an enormous responsibility, and sometimes, you are siloed in your work. A simple "How are you?" can sometimes help them see that you care about their well-being as well as their output.

The Night

There is often an immense temptation to stay up all night at two or three-day hacks. Remember, this is a choice! Don't let yourself be peer-pressured into it if you don't want to be. Sleep is essential, and sometimes a hackathon is not worth wrecking your sleep cycle.

But, if you are going to pull an all-nighter, any discomfort will be amplified further by the fact you lack sleep, so it's best to do everything in your power to avoid discomforts. Consider the following points.

Be Conscious of Your Mood

Even a single night without sleep can lead to effects such as daytime tiredness and irritability. Being around you while you're irritable can be uncomfortable and challenging, especially if you have not made others aware of how you are feeling. If you are tired, voice it! That way, others can try and be gentle with you. You're also unlikely to be the only one feeling that way, others might be comforted in knowing they are not the only ones!

It's also a good idea to pay extra attention to your conversations with your teammates; it's easy to switch into autopilot and take a negative tone. Instead, take an extra moment before speaking to ensure that you still come across cheery and positive.

For me, the most challenging time of a hack is 5 AM - I get these pinching headaches right at the front of my head. This makes me super grumpy. I always find that I'm a much nicer person if I can make it to 7 AM. If you find yourself with the same thing, stop coding, walk around, talk to people and preoccupy your mind with something else. It will pass. The only times I have ever caved and given up at hackathons is when I've tried to continue coding at this point.

Avoid the "Sugar Rush" & Alcohol

Consuming lots of sugar can get you buzzing, but a sugar low usually follows it. When you are tired and add a sugar low on top of it, there is no way you will survive the night without crashing hard. Reserve the sugar until the final sprint.

It's also best to avoid alcohol. Alcohol slows down the chemicals and pathways your brain uses to control your body. If you want to be typing at a million miles an hour, you need those pathways working at their best!

Often hackathons, especially those involving students, ban alcohol. Breaking a hackathon's code of conduct can lead to instant disqualification, so it's probably best to follow the rules!

Drink Plenty of Water

Hackathons are often huge events and are hosted in large venues. One problem with large venues - they usually have a fair amount of air conditioning. Air conditioning dries you out, so it's essential to keep yourself hydrated. It would be best if you were aiming to drink about 2 liters of water a day, so having a water bottle in front of you of a suitable size might be a helpful reminder.

Drink water as often as possible! I never drank enough, and I always felt severely dehydrated by day two. Drinking water can improve your mood and will probably make your code better.

Longer Hackathons

When the hack lasts weeks or months, keeping a consistent schedule is key. You most likely will be hacking around your studies or a day job, and it's important not to burn yourself out.

Timebox

Dedicate an hour (maximum two) a day to the hackathon. Don't be tempted to continue into the early hours of the morning. I've said it once, and I will repeat it - sleep is essential!

Don't Compromise on Downtime.

Your initial thought might be to work on the hackathon all weekend. This can negatively impact your performance across all your work as you are constantly tired. It would be best if you had dedicated time to recharge your batteries. It's also essential to ensure that your partner and friends don't feel neglected!

Power Through the Night. You've Got This!

This chapter is the last one focused on the build phase of your project. In the following chapter, we're going to talk about the project submission. We're going to learn about all the ways in which you can make your submission stand out from the rest.

The following sections are what I like to refer to as "the last push." After spending hours and hours building, your attention will be faltering. But how you present and submit your project is just as important as the code itself, don't give up now. We're getting close to the end of the hackathon journey. You've got this

CHAPTER TEN

The Submission.

You've "survived the night" and produced a project that you can be proud of - even with less sleep than usual! It's crucial to keep some energy left in the tank for this part - how your project comes across on paper is just as important as the code! This chapter focuses on the first of two significant deliverables you must submit alongside your code - the hackathon submission document. This is a high-level overview of the project - the who, what, where, and why. It is a primary resource that hackathon judges will use to determine whose project is best.

Given the significance of this document, you should consider starting it as early as possible. My suggestion is to begin this document even before starting the project itself. Throughout this book, there have been moments where I have suggested you capture experiences - this is where you want to document them. Placing them straight into the document means there is less chance of you forgetting to copy them across later. It might be best to assign a member of the team to capture experiences if you find your team forgetting.

Depending on how the hackathon is organized, the submission document may exist in a number of different places. It might be submitted through the DevPost user interface or located as a file in your code repository, for example.

Quick DevPost Tip! Devpost project submissions display in the order they are submitted. Few people know that they can edit their submissions after they submit. If you want to be top of the project gallery, submit a draft as soon as possible. Then continue to edit to your heart's content or until the deadline.

Thankfully, the submission's format remains consistent! There are several key points we need to make sure we cover. Each subheading of this section is dedicated to a subheading of your submission. To help illustrate these points I will take an example project, a fake banking app, for kids called "ThePiggyBank," which was built at a three-week-long imaginary hackathon. So let's dive straight in.

Your Introduction

Who are you? What is your project?

Your introduction is your first impression. How you word your introduction will set the tone for the rest of the document. Use an informative manner and avoid sounding casual. You can instantly make your submission look professional by incorporating your product's brand from the beginning. Start the document with your project's logo, name, and slogan. Include your elevator pitch here so that judges instantly understand your project's intentions.

We discussed "The Relational Rule" in Chapter Four - your great ideas are often those that relate to you and your team. This is hard to convey without introducing yourselves! Be sure to introduce each member of your group and what you contributed to the project. Feel free to have fun with this; you don't have to stick to your job title. If it better describes your contribution, you can refer to yourself as "The Design Dude" or "The Math Magician," for example.

Remember that this is not competitive - you are entering as a team, so don't feel the need to "one-up" your colleagues.

Section Example:

Good money habits are an essential skill in modern society. ThePiggyBank aims to educate children on money management through a gamified app experience so that they start learning about the basics of handling money/finance right away.

Meet our team:

Framing the Problem

What is the problem you are trying to solve? Who does it affect?

This section is all about helping the judges understand the problem. By getting the judges invested in the situation, they'll care more about your solution.

I always find that the best way to start this section is by asking a thought-provoking question. For example, "Have you ever thought how hard it would be to use the internet if you were blind?" or "What impact does your internet usage have on the planet?"

Once you have "sowed the seed" of the problem, use data to explain the scale of the issue. Using real data points dramatically enhances your credibility and helps convey that you know what you're talking about. Make sure to provide links to wherever this data comes from!

As mentioned in Chapter Four, keeping the problem statement related to you also helps demonstrate your own investment in this issue.

Section Example:

Experts at Cambridge University found that by age 7, 63% of children know how to count money and that you can use it to buy goods. They're also aware of what it means to earn money. However, 90% of these children have not worked out the difference between "luxuries" and "necessities." As siblings and parents, our team was worried by these findings. We want to help children form better habits from a young age, so we developed "ThePiggyBank."

Idea Explanation

What is your idea? How does it fix the problem?

Here you can really start to lay out what it is that your app actually does. Regardless of how you word this, ensure that you articulate **precisely** how your idea solves the problem you have identified.

Section Example:

"ThePiggyBank." is an educational game aimed at 5 to 10-year-olds. You are tasked with looking after "Freddy," the piggy bank's money in the game. Freddy will ask for different items, a mixture of luxuries and necessities. You, as the player, decide which of those are important to buy and see the result of your actions. Children learn that while short-term luxuries bring happiness in the moment, they are fleeting.

The app's main callout features:

- Multiple difficulty levels for children of different age groups.
- Works on all modern devices.
- Available as a website and app.

Tech Stack

How do all the pieces fit together? Does your frontend make requests to your backend? Where does your database fit in?

Give a high-level overview of what technologies come together to create your project. This can often be better explained with the aid of a diagram and a bullet-pointed list. Show how the pieces of your project talk to each other using arrows on an architecture diagram.

Section Example:

The web app was built with:

- **ReactJS** is the JavaScript library for building user interfaces
- **NextJS** is our fast React framework for performance, scalability, security, and accessibility

- **Firebase** is used to allow logins with third parties. We also used the Firestore database to store user accounts and save game data.
- **TailwindCSS** to leverage the benefits and speed of the utility-first CSS framework.
- **PhaserJS** is the 2D game framework used to create the game world.
- **NodeJS** as our backend.
- **Socket.io** for real-time updates.
- **SendGrid** for sending emails.

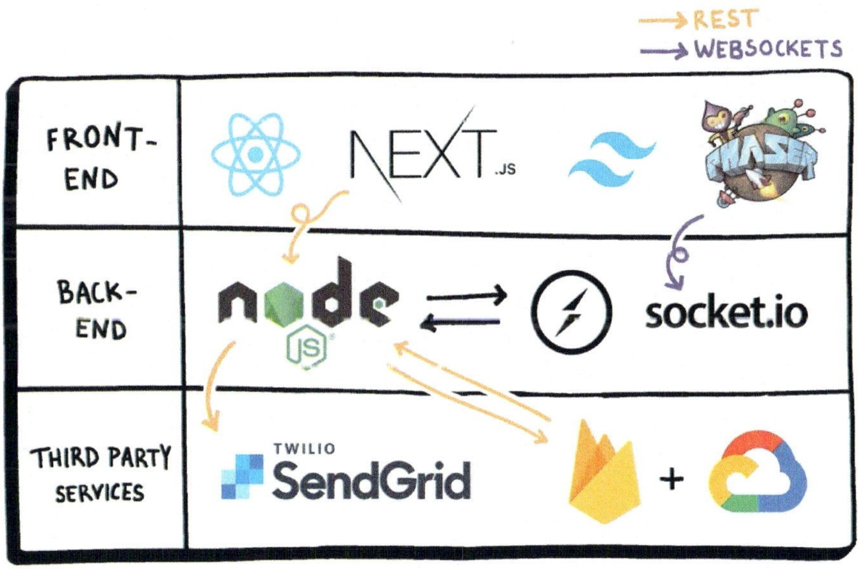

Technical Deep-Dive (Optional)

If your team completed something highly complex or technical - this is the place to let it shine. This section is a great way to show how your solution is superior when there are multiple similar solutions.

Don't avoid the detail; instead, deep-dive into how it works. You can't guarantee that the judges will ever delve into your code to find these answers for themselves, so it's better to make it unavoidable.

Your Time Usage (Optional)

It can be interesting to the judges to see how you managed your time. Give them a breakdown of where your time went and how it was distributed.

Section Example:

The work was distributed across the three weeks into four phases:

Day 1 - 4: Planning

- Project ideation
- Code structure defined and implemented
- Research into competitors
- Domain purchased

Day 5 - 13: Build

- Code code code!
- Logo created
- MVPr Completed

Day 14 - 18: Testing

- User Testing
- Improved MVPr based on feedback

Day 19 - 21: Presentation & Submission

- Demo video preparation
- Created this document!

Challenges

What was the hardest thing your team encountered? What mistakes did you make? What did you learn?

You might assume that capturing the difficulties makes you look less experienced, but this is not true. If you don't acknowledge the problems you encountered, you may give off the impression that it was easy when the reality is that you put plenty of effort into getting your project done. When capturing these challenges, try and explain what you learned from them. How would you avoid them reoccurring? This can be a great section to have everyone speak as you will all have encountered different issues.

Section Example:

Bob - "This was my first time using sockets! I've always wanted to try them but felt intimidated before now. When setting them up, we struggled for a very long time to get the connection to work even though we were pointing at the correct URL. It turns out that we had forgotten that CORS also applies to these kinds of connections..

Umar - "I really wanted to perform some user research interviews with our target user group, but due to their age, we could not perform any late at night when we were working on the project. Luckily we managed to set up some meetings with them and their parents early in the morning, but it felt rushed and too close to the end of the hackathon."

Accomplishments

What are you proud of?

It's often a good idea to call out what you're proud of alongside the challenges. Accomplishments could be high-level such as "We successfully deployed a website for the first time ever!" or something more specific such as "Managed to implement WebSockets to create real-time updates for users."

Section Example:

Over the past three weeks, we've turned an idea we thought to be impossible into a product we could actually use and potentially even monetize, while also using technology to educate young people toward a better future.

Business/Monetization Strategy (Optional)

How do you intend to make money? How much does it cost to run your project?

If you were to continue working on the project, it's essential to think about costs - nothing in this world is free! Start by focusing on how much it would cost to run your project. Look at domain and server hosting costs and try to estimate the cost per month based on different levels of demand. If you're not happy with the numbers, still be honest about them and then expand on how you would seek to reduce these costs in the future. Next, move on to how you would charge your users. This could be a one-off fee or a subscription. It's also a good idea to talk about how you will hook new users with strategies like free trials. Once you have worked out the cost of running the project and the amount you will charge your users, you can start to estimate the profit you will make. This will always be an estimate and should be called out as such.

Here we are focusing on monetizing by users paying. It should be noted that there are also other methods of monetization like business to business and ad-supported. I encourage you to research which is best for your project!

But not all hackathon projects are about making money. Some projects are more geared towards charities where your project's services will be offered for free. In this case, don't ignore this section, just focus on the cost of the platform exclusively.

This is a section that can really set submissions apart. Having a monetization strategy demonstrates that you are thinking long-term, outside the confines of the hackathon. It's something that most judges will find impressive.

Section Example:

The primary objective of ThePiggyBank is not to make money but instead to educate young people about how to form great money habits. **However,** while working on our game, we realized that there was a potential monetization strategy.

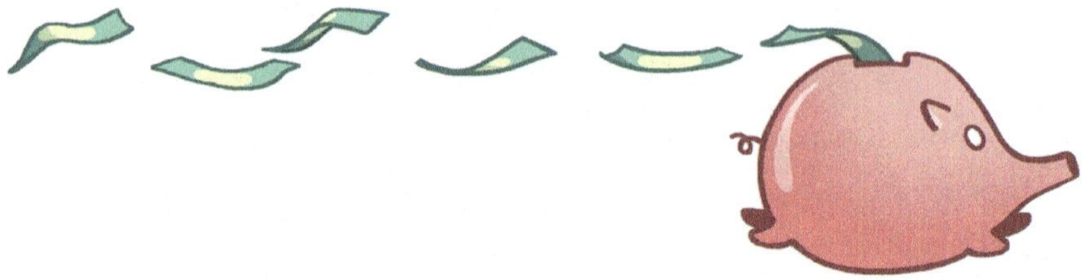

We thought we could offer the game as a subscription so that parents could sign up their children for it. We believe that parents would be keen to do this as it is an educational tool. The cost of running the servers we require for our backend and frontend services is $30 a month. By charging $5 a month to customers, we would only need six signups to cover this cost.

Next Steps

In "Next Steps" we explain where you would take the project if you had more time - how would you take the project from MVPr and MVP, to a deployed product.. One great way to structure what you would do is to talk about time frames. What would you do if you had another hackathon's worth of time? A month? A year?

If you are stuck for ideas, you might tie this section back to your challenges and talk about potential solutions you might want to investigate. Or you could look ahead to the final chapter of this book which is dedicated to what you might continue to do after the hackathon is over.

Section Example:

Although this hackathon took place over three weeks, there were still a lot of features that we would have loved to implement that we did not have time for. We intend to keep working on this project as a team after the hackathon has ended. The following is a list of some of the extensions we would like to implement next:

- The game is currently slow to load. We would love to reduce load times so that our users can get into the game faster.
- The game only has twenty levels; we want to double this number within the next month so that children have more resources to learn from.

Frequently Asked Questions (Optional)

This extra section can be great if you find yourself often being asked the same question by users while testing your hack. Answering these questions in the main body of the submission is always preferable, but there is no harm in reiterating important points via an FAQ section. If the judges are short on time, having FAQs might also act like a TL;DR (too long; didn't read) of your submission document - so keep the questions and answers short.

Video Demo

Guide the judges through a representative user journey within your project video demonstration. If judges are short on time, they may use this as the only reference instead of diving into the code - be sure to demonstrate the project at its best! Focus on the core functionality, which makes your app unique.

Here are some additional tips that are worth highlighting:

- **Avoid Boilerplate:** Avoid spending too long on the boilerplate that every app will have. A site login is common, so don't spend ages showing them how they can sign in when they already know how to sign into apps!

- **Avoid Silence:** While you are giving the tour, be sure not to leave the judges in silence! Speak over your video - describe everything that you are interacting with as you do it. Explain what is happening behind the scenes to give them added insight (especially when you are looking at a loading spinner!).
- **Cut It Down:** If your project has considerably long loading times within the journey, cut them down. If you are sneaky, you may be able to make it look like it is faster than it is.
- **No Background Music:** Avoid using background music in your video submissions. It's an added risk as you need to ensure the levels between that music and your voice are right to ensure it is not distracting - this is a waste of time.
- **Stick To Length Requirements:** Video submissions often have a length requirement ranging from two to ten mins. Always ensure that you stick to this requirement, as judges will often refrain from watching anything over the limit. Also, ensure that you are not too far below the limit, as it suggests you haven't got much to talk about. *Don't dip below thirty seconds under the submission requirement.*

DevPost note! If you submit the project via DevPost, your video submission should also include your presentation, which we will cover in the next chapter.

Project Links

A key section of any submission document is the links to your code, app, or website. This section is one of the few you might want to appear twice - at the beginning and the end of the document.

Having a link to a website can be a great way of subtly hinting to the judges that you got your project deployed and live. Always double-check your links before submitting. There is nothing worse than having the judges see a 404 page!

Submission Categories

Small hackathons will often only offer a single submission track, but at large events, you might have a choice of challenges. It might be tempting to submit your project to all tracks - don't! Judges will rarely award more than one track to the same team, so you're better to target the one that you believe your project best fits.

By highlighting a single track, you can ensure that you are hitting all of the crucial points for that challenge through your submission document.

Your Submission Checklist

After you have finished the document and are ready to submit it, consult the following checklist.

- Have you included all relevant sections in your submission?
- Have you made sure that you address all the judging criteria in your submission?
- Have you ensured it is submitted to only the most appropriate categories that it might be eligible for?
- Have you linked to your project repository and any other relevant information?

If the answer to all of the questions above is "Yes," then congratulations! Your hackathon submission is ready to be submitted. There is only one thing left on your to-do list - the presentation. In the next chapter, we will explore what makes a great slide deck and some public speaking tips.

With your submission in, you only have one more deliverable to worry about - the presentation. The best part is that you have already completed all of the content you'll need without realizing it. Your presentation is a guided tour of your submission, and as such, all your slide content can be ported directly from your submission document.

It's crucial to convey the wonderful information from your submission, but you have some other goals here too! You want to emphasize your confidence and belief in your product but also demonstrate how your team worked together. These goals are far easier to sow into the minds of the judges when presenting. This chapter will focus on three main parts of presentations - the slide deck, message delivery, and public speaking tips.

Slide Deck Structure

Your presentation will never be long enough to cover your entire submission. At a minimum, use the available time to convey the project and hit all judging criterion. The smallest example presentation would probably contain the following slides:

- Intro
- Meet the team
- Framing the problem
- Idea explanation
- (Slide here for each judging criteria)
- Thanks & questions

Remember to also include your demo in there! This works best after the idea explanation or the judging criteria slides. Usually, you'll have it ready on the same computer and navigate to it at the appropriate point in the presentation.

So what do we mean by slides for judging criteria? Judging criteria are the model with which they will score your project. You want to ensure that judges can't miss that you have hit all the requirements, so they give you a high score. Dedicating a slide to each criterion makes it easy for judges to check these criteria off. In Chapter One, we provided business value, monetization strategy, implementation, realistic capability, and presentation as examples of judging criteria. The presentation criterion can be omitted, as the whole of this deck will count towards it. However, all the others can have a slide dedicated to them:

- Business value can be inferred through your idea explanation slide but don't forget to emphasize it.
- Monetization strategy criteria could be addressed using maths straight from the relevant submission section.

- Implementation criteria could be hit by adding your tech stack as a slide.
- Realistic capability criteria could be hit by adding a URL for the audience to go and try your application or website. If it is deployed, no one can argue it isn't realistic!

Beware! Don't just create a slide with a title that matches the criteria, as this can seem a little too tryhard. Instead, have your content allow the judges to infer that you have hit the criteria.

Given additional time (and if they are not already necessary to hit the criteria), you can include the following presentation expansions:

- Tech stack
- Challenges you faced
- What you're proud of
- Business/Monetization Strategy
- Next steps

The judges will probably see hundreds of slides throughout the hackathon presentations, so make yours stand out from the crowd by including your branding assets throughout the deck. Create a slide deck template with your brand colors and fonts, and be sure your logo is in the corner of every slide.

Getting the Message Across

In martial arts, it's common practice to treat a weapon as an extension of yourself - the same could be said about your slide deck. You want people to focus on what you're saying, so use your slide deck to draw their focus further into your words, not distract from them. Let's look at a few tips:

- Keep it big and bold. Keep your slide deck interesting by using a variety of font sizes and weights. Double your font weights between your paragraph and title text.
- Avoid text-heavy slides. Keep the word count down wherever possible. If you feature lots of text on your slides, you will find that the audience will try and read it all instead of listening to you speak. A good rule is to summarise your content on the slide and use your words to expand upon the summaries.
- Interact with your audience where possible. It can be hard to concentrate on one person talking if there isn't any interaction. Ask questions to the audience and get their hands up. E.g., Using the example from our Chapter Ten, "Hand up if you have a younger sibling... Keep your hand up if you believe they do not understand money management." If possible, the audience can feel more invested in the idea if you let them try out your demo.
- Alternate speakers. Presenting can be a very nerve-wracking experience, so divide and conquer! Each team member should take a section of the presentation to own. This keeps things interesting for the audience as they won't spend the whole time listening to the same person. It also demonstrates team collaboration which is a key goal to convey in the presentation. To avoid this being jarring for the viewers, call out when it is about to happen.

- Allow them to explore for more. Due to time constraints, you may not have time to cover every submission area. So instead, call out the headline and direct readers to your submission if they want to learn more. E.g., "We ran into several challenges during the hackathon, including X, Y, and Z. You can read more about these in our submission document."

Now that you have the perfect slide deck, let's turn our attention to making the delivery awesome!

Public Speaking Tips

Remember that you are the presentation, not the slides! So let's make sure you come across as confident and in control. Consider the following:

- Project! Make sure that when you start speaking, the audience can hear you. A simple - "Can everybody hear me okay?" can work as a nice little ice breaker.
- Go 10% slower than what you think is the right speed. Most people have a tendency to speed up during presentations. When they do, they fill the inevitable pauses with words such as "like" or "um." You give your mind time to think and become calmer and more collected in your delivery by slowing down.

- Keep things moving. Try not to linger on one slide for more than a couple of minutes; keep the visuals interesting for your audience. If something is complex and requires more time, consider splitting it across multiple slides.
- Don't prepare your pitch word for word. Instead, bullet point the notes you need to hit and tie them together on the fly. This will make your presentation sound more natural when you come to deliver it as you aren't reading from a script.
- Practice makes perfect. Rehearsing your pitch will make your final delivery look all the more prepared. Take half an hour and run through each person's part. Be sure to provide constructive feedback to each other so that you can improve.
- Don't cower behind your laptop. Where possible, let someone else handle the slide transitions so you can stand up and use your hands for emphasis. Even better, use a clicker!

Humor can also be an excellent thing to bring into the presentation. In the foreword of this book, I mentioned an app called "Spidentify" which used image recognition to identify dangerous animals. The app had one little flaw, though. It would always match a photo as an animal, even if it wasn't one. During the presentation, instead of hiding this flaw, we highlighted it. We gave the app a photo of Donald Trump, and when he was classified as a snake, the room erupted with laughter. Perhaps there is a limitation from your submission document that could be equally amusing?

Your Presentation Checklist

Consult the following checklist after you have finished the presentation document and are ready to start practicing:

- Does your deck demonstrate that you have hit all the judging criteria?
- Does every member of your team have a part to play in the presentation?
- Is your branding present throughout the deck?
- Are all the slides simple and easy to read?

If the answer to all of the questions above is "Yes," then congratulations! Your presentation deck is ready to be used. Get practicing and remain confident as your deck will surely knock it out of the park.

A small boost of confidence!

Public speaking can be really daunting. If the idea of having to speak in front of a large group of people is freaking you out, I wanted to offer one small word of encouragement - No one in the room knows your project better than you and your team. Therefore, you are the most knowledgeable people in the room on the subject.

That's All, Folks! Or Is It?

With this chapter complete, we have covered everything from the process and ways of working to the toolkit and creative edge to make your hackathon project stand out from the crowd. But the journey does not have to end just because the hackathon has! In the final chapter, we will talk about what you can do while you are waiting to hear the verdict and what you can do to take your project further.

CHAPTER TWELVE

NEXT STEPS

Before we get into this chapter, there is one thing you've got to do - rest and recover! Hackathons can be physically and mentally exhausting. This chapter can wait until you've taken a big sigh, had a good night's sleep, reflected on your experience, eaten a warm meal, called your loved ones, told them you're not dead, et cetera, et cetera.

This chapter is dedicated to all things post-hack. We will talk about different post-hack activities you can occupy yourself with while waiting to hear the verdict. We will then discuss how best to handle the result when it is announced. The focus of this chapter is to ensure you set yourself up so that the hackathon experience doesn't end when the event does, and your learnings carry you forward into future endeavors.

Post-Hack Activities

This section contains a bundle of post-hack activities that you can complete in your own time - no more racing against the clock! But sometimes, the time between presenting your project and hearing the result can feel like forever. If you're looking for something to keep yourself occupied with until you hear the news, here you go!

Compliment Your Colleagues

You've spent the length of the event getting to know some great people. If someone taught you something new or went above and beyond to keep your team motivated, then be sure to call this out and thank them.

Equally, if something didn't work well, you can provide some constructive feedback to the individual or group. It's best to avoid engaging in this activity until everyone has recovered.

Reflect on Your Learnings

Hopefully, you've had some time to think through your entire hackathon experience. Looking back, what would you have changed? What went really well? What was your highlight? This activity can take whatever form you like; you can think it through in your head out on a walk or write it down. While it is great to explore this independently, it can also be a positive team activity as your teammates will probably have contrasting experiences.

Once you've found your learnings, revisit them before attending future events so you can do more of what went well and hopefully avoid any pitfalls. And, if you're feeling brave, you can also publish these learnings publicly. The hackathon organizers will appreciate this content as it helps get their event out there and it also allows others to learn from your experience.

Learning in public is one of the most rewarding things I have ever undertaken. In tech, it's easy to work on a side project and not receive recognition, especially from friends and family who don't necessarily understand what you're working on. By sharing in the public domain, you can receive encouragement from anywhere in the world! If you're unsure where to start, posting on Medium is a great place to start.

Update Your Projects List

Hackathons are one of the fastest ways to create projects. If you feel like your portfolio doesn't have much content, you can fix this quickly by including your hackathon projects on your website or in the projects section of your LinkedIn profile.

If you have a personal website, you could dedicate a page to each hackathon project you participate in. You don't need to write any new content for this page, as you can copy and paste from your submission documentation and even link to your presentation if it was recorded. Be sure to include links to the demo if you managed to get it deployed! If not, then pack the page full of screenshots.

Share with Your Network

LinkedIn and Twitter are great platforms to share your project with a like-minded audience. Share your experiences with the technologies you used and share the demo.

You never know who might read your post, and that's half the fun - while posting about a hackathon project called "InterviewToast" on LinkedIn, I was contacted by the CEO of symbl.ai, whose APIs we were using as part of the application. He'd tried out our demo and was interested in finding out more!

Build on Your project

You might feel like you have struck gold with your project! Perhaps you can see the project turning into the next million-dollar startup similar to those we explored in the Chapter One. If this is the case, don't lose momentum! Keep meeting with the team and try and get into the habit of regularly improving the project through small iterations.

Local meetups are a perfect next step. Find a meetup related to the technology you have used and present your idea to the community.

Don't Do These

While keeping yourself busy is necessary, don't make these little mistakes. They might cost you the competition!

Don't Work on the "O.G." Codebase

Be careful not to tarnish the existing code base when building on the project while judging is still ongoing! If the project is being judged and you are seen to be working on it past the deadline, it could invalidate your submission. Instead, fork your code into a new repository to continue your work.

Don't Review the Project Gallery

This point is controversial. It reflects only my personal experience with these events. Take it with a grain of salt!

In highly competitive hackathons, try and avoid the competition. Hearing about other teams' projects can make you feel less optimistic about your own submission. Instead, wait until the judging is over before investigating other projects.

Don't Dwell on It

If the event's judging concludes days or weeks later, avoid thinking about it too much. While waiting to hear the news, it's easy to let the nerves consume everything. Recognize that you have done all you can now. Expending extra energy overthinking things won't help you or those around you.

Admittedly this is something I find very hard to do myself. My partner always finds it difficult to engage with me while I wait to hear the news. The only thing that works for me is occupying my mind with another tech project. Keep my mind focused elsewhere.

I'M SO NERVOUS. DO YOU THINK WE DID ENOUGH?
DON'T FOCUS ON THAT NOW. LOOK AT THE FIREWORKS!

The Verdict

The moment has come. Judging has concluded, and the winners are about to be announced. Regardless of what happens, there are some things you really should try and do.

Recognize Your Achievement

You have dedicated time and a mountain of energy to building something from nothing. You've most likely made some new friends that you'll keep in contact with. You might have found some new skills, and you've probably discovered a new definition for the word "tired."

This hackathon would not have been the same without you, and you should leave with your head held high whatever happens.

Try and Get Feedback

Whether you win or lose, feedback from the judges can be invaluable. If you are not automatically given any feedback, try and pull a judge aside and ask some of the following questions:

- What was the highlight of our project?
- What do you think we could have done better?
- If you could wave a magic wand and change one thing, what would you change?

If judges are not available to you for some reason, ask your fellow competitors!

When You Miss the Mark

If today wasn't your day and you didn't win the hack, I want you to revisit your learnings from the beginning of this chapter. I bet that there are things on that list that are more valuable than any money. Hackathons are experiences like no other, and I'm hoping you can take your newfound hacking expertise and apply it to other parts of your life.

How to be a great runner-up:

- **Congratulate the winners:** There's nothing quite as cool as calmly walking up to the winners, shaking them by the hand, and congratulating them on their win. Be this person.
- **Keep spirits high:** Other members of your team might not be taking the loss as well as you, try and be the one to keep spirits high. Remind the group of what they have achieved and the fun they have had.
- **Prepare for future victory:** With every hackathon you attend, you'll gain more experience. You'll be able to practice and put these ways of working into practice and lead future teams to success.

Remember that hackathons take many different formats. If you come out of the event feeling down about the whole thing, maybe you just haven't found the format that works best for you. Your next hackathon is just a sign-up away, so what are you waiting for?

If You Win

Congratulations! Winning a hackathon is no small feat. You and your team should be proud of what you have accomplished.

How to be a great winner:

- **Remember it was a team effort:** You couldn't have won without the help of your team. If you talk about your role in the project, mention that it "was a small piece in a large puzzle." To quote Thomas Merton - "Humility is the surest sign of strength."
- **Remain humble:** While you will be ecstatic, you'll be surrounded by people that missed the mark. A little courtesy will earn you a lot of respect.
- **Congratulate other attendees:** Praise attendees on their achievements. If there was something that stood out to you or made you go "wow" be sure to let them know.
- **Thank the organizers for throwing this all together:** there would be no event without them after all.

Keep your hackathon momentum going. If you have seen gold at this level, why not try raising the stakes to national or even international hackathons? If you can't go any higher, than maybe now is the time to start teaching?

Final Thoughts

Writing this book was like attending a hackathon. It started with problem statements - "How can I encourage and help those attending hackathons for the first time?" And "how can I help those that already attend hackathons perform better?". We had criteria. We wanted a book accessible to all, effortless to read, and easy to reference. As a team, we went through many ideation sessions before deciding to write the book you are reading. We created ways of working to help us get to our goal quickly. We performed market research and user testing to ensure that what you read represents our best work. We iterated. And now, you get to judge the book.

The point is that the ways of working, tools, and processes we have identified in this book can be used at hackathons wherever you might find them. Because they will crop up in the places you least expect them.

Wishing you every success in your hackathon adventures,

P.S. This book is a self-published passion project created by a small group of friends. If you've enjoyed reading the book and want to help us out, the most impactful thing you can do for us is spread the word. We'll let you ideate on how you think you can do that best. You should be a pro at ideation by now!

About the Author

Hi, my name's Sam Larsen-Disney.

I've spent most of my life in Brighton, UK. I studied Computer Science with Artificial Intelligence at King's College London University. It was here I was first introduced to the world of hackathons. I started my career in R&D at American Express, I've since bounced around companies large and small.

Nowadays, I am based in London. I'm a full-time software engineer and passionate hackathon enthusiast. I have attended over 50+ hackathons as an attendee, mentor, or sponsor and won over $20,000 in 2021. I currently work for Amplitude, a job I got at a hackathon. I have always enjoyed teaching other people, and this book is my way of giving back to the hackathon community.

I met Irma in France at age fifteen – never in my wildest dreams did I think we would be creating a book together 12 years on.

About the Illustrator

Hi, my name's Irma Van den Poel.

My main jam is illustration and creating comics. I believe comics and pictures are the best way to go when you want people to absorb and learn. Sam and I have managed to find the perfect mixture of fun and learning with this book!

I studied Graphic Storytelling at The Animation Workshop in Denmark, and now I've moved back to my home country of Sweden, Stockholm to work as a freelancing artist. In between drawing I write comic manuscripts, sew costumes and sing in a choir.

As for hackathons, Sam was the one to introduce me to them. After creating this book, I've gone from a complete novice to really appreciating this exciting part of the wonderful world of technology.

What will you build?

Printed in Great Britain
by Amazon

82118405R00093